STATISTICS
FOR
EDUCATORS

Michael John Horvath, EdD

SPECIAL CHILD PUBLICATIONS / SEATTLE

Special Child Publications
J. B. Preston, Editor & Publisher
P. O. Box 33548
Seattle, Washington 98133

Serving the special child since 1962.

International Standard Book Number: 0-87562-084-1

94 93 92 91 90 89 88 87 86 85
10   9   8   7   6   5   4   3   2   1

CONTENTS

PREFACE

This text is the outgrowth of techniques developed over several years to teach test statistics to people who blanched when the term *statistics* was mentioned and who believed that testing was performed to comply with state and federal regulations, but rarely had any value in teaching. The audience for this book includes preservice and inservice educators in special education and educational psychology, and anyone asked to serve on a multidisciplinary team as mandated by Public Law 94-142 or similar state laws. Educators in undergraduate, graduate, and inservice courses in clinical or diagnostic-prescriptive teaching, diagnosis, tests and measurements, methods, overviews of educational psychology, counseling parents, and writing IEPs may find this text appropriate. Administrators, regular education teachers, social workers, and school nurses may wish to use this for review and reference.

In this book, the emphasis is on conceptual understanding and practical application of descriptive statistics used in the diagnostic-prescriptive approach to educational intervention. The value of standardized testing in this process is presented with the objective of showing how to use assessment data to effect positive educational programming. Case studies are used to illustrate the process from referral data through the construction of an IEP.

To accomplish the objectives of understanding and using testing efficiently, we decided to depart from contemporary approaches. Texts on statistics are often incomprehensible to the educator because the language is "numbers" rather than conceptual narrative, the use is often research-oriented rather than program-oriented, and notation may be complicated and jargon heavy-handed. Conversely, texts for educators on testing are often simplistic in their description of test statistics and of little use in the selection, interpretation, and explanation of tests and the subsequent integration of test data into viable educational prescriptions.

The fourteen chapters of this book can be divided into six sections. Chapter 1 offers guidelines on the purpose and content of test reports, including psychological reports. Four case studies are presented. Chapter 2 offers an overview of the testing process. Chapters 3 through 10 review the statistics of testing, including test construction. Chapters 11 and 12 summarize the testing process and provide case studies for review. Chapter 13 depicts the construction of an IEP using formal and informal assessment data with a case study. Finally, Chapter 14 offers help in the explanation of data to parents and others through the use of a case study.

CHAPTER 1

THE MUMBO-JUMBO OF TEST REPORTS

A good psychological report is a useful tool to the people who provide educational services to children. Increasingly, the psychologist has been expected to function as part of a multidisciplinary team. The team's mission is to provide educational programming relevant to the needs of the children they serve. Now it is no longer justifiable to perform extensive psychological testing solely for the purpose of labeling a child. The expectation is that some useful programming information will be included as part of each diagnosis. For purposes of individualization of instruction, testing has come to be regarded as an integral part of the teaching process.

Many teachers are reluctant to use psychological reports in their teaching because they feel that the information gained is not worth the effort and time spent to acquire it. Some feel that the suggestions made cannot be realistically implemented in the classroom. Other teachers don't read psychological reports because their school systems may have a policy against releasing the reports to teachers. These practices are unfortunate because they are violative of the spirit of the multidisciplinary team approach.

Both teachers and psychologists have been asked to take on new responsibilities. Teachers should know how to translate the results of testing into educational programming. To do that most efficiently, a teacher must know how to read a psychological report for relevant information. Psychologists are responsible for writing good reports. An outline is presented below.

The Psychological Report

Several formats for writing psychological reports exist. One that is representative was developed by Winifred Kirk. It is divided into nine sections.

Section one. This is demographic data. A representative form is presented.

Name_____Parent_____
Address_____Telephone_____
Age_____DOB_____Date of Test_____
Sex_____Grade_____School_____
Teacher_____Referred by_____
Date of Report_____Examiner_____

Section two. This has to do with the reason the child was referred for testing. Some people call this the presenting problem. It is a brief, specific statement of the educational and/or behavioral problem or problems the child is experiencing. "Possible special education" is assumed and is therefore a meaningless statement. "Johnny is having problems in school" is not explicit enough. "Johnny is having difficulty in language arts activities" is better. "Johnny is having difficulty forming letters and numbers, drawing pictures, and coloring" is a brief, explicit statement which is educationally relevant. It gives the examiner a great deal of information which does not have to be discovered during testing. This is more efficient because the examiner can select tests which will zero-in on the problem. It also provides a statement which can be confirmed or denied for the child's present teacher. Finally, this statement provides a starting point for informal testing which may be the responsibility of the special education teacher. A more specific statement here usually leads to more useful test information later.

Section three. This is a report of background information. Only observable facts should be presented. This is not the place for conclusions, gossip, third-party statements unless the sources are quoted, value judgments, highly confidential material, or anything not relevant to the educational process. In a few rare cases, relevant material may come to light in the form of rumors or undocumented observations. These may be included, but must be identified as such, for example, "sibling report of erratic sleep patterns," "rumor of gang membership," or "teacher report of possible child abuse."

This section may be subdivided into family background, physical and developmental history, and school history. The family background subsection may contain information on the family constellation, environmental conditions, emotional stability, intellectual interests, economic status, parental interest, type of discipline, and family unity if relevant. The objective is to find any problems, such as frequent moves, which may be hindering the child educationally.

The physical and developmental history subsection may contain information on physical problems (if any), approximate times the child learned to manipulate objects, sit, walk, talk, etc. Included also, may be a statement on how the child reacted to people, books, toys, and television at various ages. Any traumatic experiences or sudden changes in behavior should be noted.

The school history subsection may include information on what age a child started school, if there was a preschool experience, what the attendance pattern has been, when problems were first noted, what efforts were made to alleviate problems, what results those efforts yielded, and what kind of classes were previously attended—large/small, slow/fast, group/individual, and so on. It is helpful to include the types of curricula, methods, and materials used, if available.

Section four. This section details prior testing. The history of test performance is sometimes very important. Curricular changes may place new burdens on the child with which she cannot cope. These can show up in the test history and provide clues regarding learning styles or successful/unsuccessful methodologies. Teachers will often skip this section or get lost in the mumbo-jumbo of the terminology and statistics used in this and the following section. If these two sections are not understood, there is no way to tell if the conclusions and recommendations the examiner gives are justified by the testing. Explanations of the statistics of testing may be found throughout chapters of this book.

Section five. In this section, present testing information is listed. Included are chronological age (CA) at the time the test was administered, total test scores, and subtest scores. Many teachers do not understand all the different ways scores can be reported. To avoid confusion, it is important that scores be reported in as many ways as possible. The ideal situation exists when a score is reported in at least the standard form, as a percentile, and as a grade and/or age equivalent. Each of these terms is explained in later chapters.

Section six. Clinical observations made during the evaluation process are reported here. This is a brief and objective report of traits such as test behavior, reaction to stress, emotional involvement, hidden abilities, relevant personal assets and deficits, and motivation. The examiner is trying to convey a feeling for the child and his problems. Many times there will not be enough of this kind of data to justify a separate section. In that case, observatons may be reported in the following section.

Section seven. This is the interpretation of test results. It is the job of the examiner to provide an interpretation of why the child performed as she did. Included here should be a theoretical explanation of the child's behavior. It is important, however, for the examiner to remember that the report must be understandable to its consumers to be useful. The primary consumers should be the people who work most directly with children—the teachers. They will want to know what the tests used evaluate, and how the results are relevant to educational programming. The relevant questions here are: Do the results tell a story? Can the symptoms be grouped into educational syndromes? Can the interpretation be justified?

Section eight. Here a summary and diagnosis are presented. Material from all previous sections is used to draw educationally relevant conclusions regarding the child's academic and social competence. If inconsistencies exist, they should be pointed out and interpreted. A review of the presenting problem, relevant information, formal and informal test observations, and theoretical interpretation of results are used to support the diagnostic conclusion.

Section nine. This final section is composed of recommendations. It is here that educationally relevant solutions to deal with the presenting problem are proposed. These should be both specific and useful. Methods and materials should be suggested. Activities which would help the child to overcome his problems should be detailed. In these recommendations, it is very important to prescribe realistic activities for the classroom, resource room, or home. It borders on the unethical to recommend a remedial program which is based on questionable research and which is too time-consuming or impractical for a teacher or parent to manage.

In this kind of framework, it is most efficient for the teacher and psychologist to work together in the evaluation process. Psychologists should learn specific methods and materials and teachers should be responsible for some testing. In this way, each will think of the other as a partner on the multidisciplinary team; such a collaboration can only lead to improved educational services for children. The teacher and psychologist should complement each other professionally, rather than pursuing the adversarial relationship which can exist if there is little communication between them.

READING THE REPORT

Four psychological reports will be presented. The first two need major revisions to be useful in providing educationally relevant services to the children. The second two reports as written are much more useful. A critique follows each report in the form of unanswered questions and some discussion where necessary.

Psychological Report 1

NAME: James Cruz   **PARENT:** Hector Cruz
ADDRESS: **TELEPHONE:**
AGE: 14–1   **DOB:** 1/19/67   **DATE OF TEST:** 2/17/81
SEX: M   **GRADE:** 7   **SCHOOL:** Johnson
TEACHER: Joan Martin   **REFERRED BY:** teacher
DATE OF REPORT: 2/25/81   **EXAMINER:** George Nagy

EDUCATIONAL HISTORY:

James has attended five schools in seven years. He came to Johnson at the beginning of this year.

TESTS ADMINISTERED:

Arithmetic

OK in arithmetic, subtraction, multiplication, and division, unable to do fractions, has memorized multiplication tables.

Reading

Silvaroli Informal Reading Test (Oral Reading Levels)

     Reading Independent Level 2 – 3
     Reading Instructional Level 4

Reading Frustration Level 5
Listening Comprehension Level 5

Reads below grade level. Will need help in reading selections in regular classes.

Woodcock

Reading Grade Score 5.2
Easy Reading Level 4.1
Failure Level 7.8

Very weak in Passage Comprehension (3.8) and Word Attack (4.7).

Visual-Motor

Bender-Gestalt indicates development at the 7 to 7½ year old level. This indicates difficulties in the areas of visual-motor integration. Errors in rotation and distortion of shape are noted; figures often impulsively done.

Forms Completed:

	YES	NO
Lunch	....	....
Health	....	....

CONCLUSION:

This student needs remedial reading instruction.

This is a rather poor psychological report. Testing has taken precedence over evaluation. This violates the purpose of a psychological report, which is to assemble and interpret useful data. Administering tests as an end in itself is not correct and this examiner has confused testing with evaluation. A number of questions have been left unanswered:

— Why is the student being referred for testing?
— Is there anything in the developmental history to indicate problems?
— Is English the dominant home language?
— What about attendance patterns and types of classes?
— Is learning valued at home?
— What previous testing has been done, if any?
— What is the child's IQ?
— How does the examiner know that the student is competent in the operations of addition, subtraction, multiplication, and division?
— How did the examiner learn of difficulty with fractions or that the student knows his multiplication tables?
— Could a different examiner have interpreted the arithmetic data differently?
— In reading, what are the subtest scores?
— Why are stanine, percentile, and standard scores missing?
— Why were two reading tests given? Does one test duplicate the results of the other?
— What are the test observations?

- Was the student anxious or unmotivated to the point that test scores could have been affected?
- Were there language problems?
- Is the fact that the child performed below grade level significant?
- How does one know when a score is significant?
- On what basis have the interpretations been made?
- What does the visual-motor information mean?
- What is visual-motor integration in educational terms (i.e., what can and can not the student do?
- What is rotation and distortion of shape? Is this significant? How?
- Do the symptoms group themselves into syndromes?
- What support is there for the conclusion?
- Is the visual-motor information significant enough to be used in the conclusion?
- What recommendations come from this data?
- How can this child be helped?

Psychological Report 2

NAME: Jill Ann Smith   **PARENT:** James Smith
ADDRESS: **TELEPHONE:**
AGE: 9–7   **DOB:** 3/17/71   **DATE OF TEST:** 10/14/80
SEX: F   **GRADE:** 4   **SCHOOL:** Coolidge
TEACHER: Mary Adams   **REFERRED BY:** teacher
DATE OF REPORT: 11/17/80   **EXAMINER:** Aaron Blue

REASON FOR REFERRAL:

Academic. Jill is hyperactive and immature.

BACKGROUND INFORMATION:

Jill comes from a home with a broken family. Her mother is a waitress in a bar and associates with persons of disreputable character. Her father is an alcoholic. Two older children live at home and are unsupervised. The social worker reports that Jill is spoiled.

PREVIOUS TESTING:

Otis Lennon	4/3/78	IQ = 76
Slosson Intelligence Test	5/16/78	IQ = 87

PRESENT TESTING:

Intelligence

WISC–R

Verbal	SS	Performance	SS
Information	7	Picture Completion	9
Similarities	9	Picture Arrangement	8
Arithmetic	8	Block Design	9

Vocabulary	11	Object Assembly	8
Comprehension	11	Coding	11
(Digit Span)	8		

Verbal IQ   95   Performance IQ   92

Full Scale IQ   92

Achievement

WRAT	Grade Level
Oral Word Recognition	4.7
Spelling	4.7
Arithmetic	3.9

Visual-Motor

Bender-Gestalt

Developmental Age: 7.0 to 7.5 (Below Average)

OBSERVATIONS:

Jill was an active, yet cooperative, right-handed young lady. At times her interest in the testing situation would falter. She seemed to be daydreaming a lot and was easily distracted. Because rapport was easy to establish, all test results appear to be valid.

TEST RESULTS:

Past tests indicate a great deal of fluctuation in IQ scores. This may stem from emotional blocks brought about by an unstable home environment. Her present performance puts her in the average range of intelligence. The Verbal scores were only slightly higher than the Performance scores. There was only moderate scatter among most of the individual test scores. Strong areas included vocabulary and verbal comprehension on the Verbal scale and simple substitution using paper and pencil on the Performance scale. Weaknesses were noted in knowledge of basic factual information and on inability to think abstractly.

The WRAT indicates that she is functioning at the expected level academically. Several errors were marginal.

Her performance on the Bender was below level. The errors appeared to be in the area of visual-motor integration rather than perception.

SUMMARY AND DIAGNOSIS:

Jill at this time appears average in her mental development. School achievement was equal to mental development. Other tests indicate that auditory and visual attention skills are weak. Another problem is visual-motor integrative skills. Her performance on tasks involving the manipulation of visual and aural stimuli through oral and written responses was low.

RECOMMENDATIONS:

An LD evaluation is in order to determine the most appropriate program for Jill.

This report is a definite improvement over the first. There are still questions which can be asked throughout:

- What does the writer mean by hyperactive and immature?
- What are the behavioral indicators?
- How is the background information relevant to the presenting problem educationally?
- What is the purpose of including value judgments and unsupported statements?

In light of questionable reliability, validity, and possible difficulty in interpretation, the reader would not necessarily have great faith in the scores reported in the past testing section. Was this all that was available?

Are any of the IQ scores significantly above or below normal? Are the *Wide Range Achievement Test* (WRAT) scores within the normal range? How can one tell? If any of the results of the WRAT are significant, further testing in that area should have been performed. The WRAT is a screening test which will point out areas of weakness, but was not designed to be used for in-depth evaluation.

How does one know if the developmental age score on the *Bender-Gestalt* test is below average?

What techniques did the examiner use to keep Jill's attention focused on the task at hand? Could the testing environment have had anything to do with this?

With IQ tests, an identical numerical score on two different tests may indicate different functioning levels. This is true with the *Wechsler Intelligence Scale for Children-Revised* (WISC-R) and the *Slosson Intelligence Test* (SIT). There are three reasons that this happens. Different constructs may have been used as a basis for building the test, or the standard deviation of the two tests are different, or the error in one is greater than that of another. In this case, if the same test had been used throughout, earlier results may not appear to have been so different.

What is the significance of discrepancy and scatter? How does one know what strengths and weaknesses were present? What is simple substitution? How can the test results be interpreted in terms of specific performance (theoretical interpretation)?

On the WRAT, how does one know that Jill is functioning at the expected level? Should other achievement testing have been done?

What is the meaning of the *Bender-Gestalt* interpretation? What does this indicate in terms of the educationally relevant competencies the child may or may not possess?

In the summary and diagnosis section, other nonreported test results are used to indicate deficient performance. This is not the place to introduce new material. Can these conclusions be justified? A number of terms were used. What do they mean educationally and/or behaviorally?

What activities, curricula, methods, or materials can the teacher use to help this student? Why is learning disability a sudden consideration? Was any indication given earlier? Why didn't the examiner do at least some of that learning disability evaluation? Is the examiner labeling the student learning disabled?

Psychological Report 3

NAME: Audri Green   **PARENT:** Samuel Green
ADDRESS: **TELEPHONE:**
AGE: 8–6   **DOB:** 5/24/72   **DATE OF TEST:** 11/11/80
SEX: F   **GRADE:** 3   **SCHOOL:** Walker
TEACHER: Rhoda Caspar   **REFERRED BY:** teacher
DATE OF REPORT: 12/2/80   **EXAMINER:** Joseph Burgdorf

PRESENTING PROBLEM:

Audri has reversals in writing, often writes right to left, has poor phonics, a limited vocabulary, has trouble following oral directions, has fragmented verbalizations, and often can't remember the alphabet. She often doesn't attend, yet has a good attitude and is positive about herself and the school experience.

BACKGROUND INFORMATION:

Audri's mother is a legal secretary and her father is an accountant. Both expressed concern for Audri's low achievement. A normal developmental history has been reported—Audri rolled over at 2½ months, said her first word at 8 months, walked at 11 months, and was speaking in sentences by 30 months. No traumatic experiences were reported. Audri attended kindergarten at Northside and first and second grades at Walker.

PREVIOUS TESTING:

Prior to this there has been no standardized testing on Audri. On the district screening instrument given in first grade, nothing unusual was apparent.

PRESENT TESTING:

Intelligence: WISC–R

Verbal	*Performance*
Information	Picture Completion
Similarities	Picture Arrangement*
Arithmetic	Block Design
Vocabulary*	Object Assembly
Comprehension*	Coding*
(Digit Span)*	
	* Indicates below-average scoring
Verbal IQ 91	Performance IQ 93

Full Scale IQ   91

Achievement

WRAT	%ile	Grade	SS
Reading	19	2.4	87
Spelling	12	1.9	82
Arithmetic	10	1.8	81

Scores in Spelling and Arithmetic are below average.

Woodcock Reading Mastery Tests

Poor auditory memory and visualization skills (e.g., letter reversals) hinder comprehension.

Keymath Diagnostic Arithmetic Test

No arithmetic strengths are apparent. Audri does not seem to grasp the concepts underlying arithmetic processes. She is far behind.

Perceptual

ITPA

Scores on the subtests of Auditory Reception, Auditory-Vocal Association, Auditory Sequential Memory, and Visual-Sequential Memory were below normal. The Manual Expression score was high normal.

CLINICAL OBSERVATIONS:

Audri was willing to cooperate, even though a task was extremely distasteful. She once stated that she always worked hard because learning took a lot of effort. Her anxiety at times seemed to interfere with her test performance.

TEST RESULTS:

A number of presenting problems were listed. Audri's scores on the IQ test were within the normal range. This indicates that she has the intellectual potential to cope with the requirements of the normal class. Audri scored below the normal range in the WISC–R subtests of Comprehension and Digit Span, indicating difficulty with auditory memory. This is consistent with her difficulties in following directions, using phonics, and remembering the alphabet. Because of difficulty on the Coding, Vocabulary, and Comprehension subtests, one would suspect reading problems. Audri scored in the low normal range on reading measures.

On an informal test, Audri was asked to describe a picture "in her mind's eye." She was unable to accomplish this. This lack of adequate visualization skills, plus her poor auditory memory skills, are a factor in her academic difficulties.

The WRAT scores indicate below average performance in spelling and arithmetic. Reading performance was borderline. KeyMath scores were all depressed, although the Arithmetic subtest score of the WISC–R placed her in the average range. Perhaps fatigue was operating in this situation. During the Woodcock test she often asked the examiner to repeat directions and stimuli. Letter reversals affected her pronunciation of words and consequently, her comprehension. Low auditory subtest scores on the ITPA further confirm problems in the auditory modality. Memory seems to be a problem.

SUMMARY AND DIAGNOSIS:

Audri has the intelligence to cope with the regular curriculum. She exhibited difficulties with auditory memory and visualization. Attention span problems, perhaps caused in part by fatigue, may have helped to depress test scores.

At this time, placement in a learning disability program is warranted.

RECOMMENDATIONS:

Help is needed in every academic activity. The key may be to find a method for learning. Use of a multimodal approach such as that proposed by Fernald might help.

Concrete manipulatives should be considered as a teaching strategy. As many listening and memory activities as possible should be used.

This report is of far better quality than the two preceding it. The examiner has grouped subtest scores together to confirm psychoeducational problems. Often, a causal factor will become apparent during this theoretical interpretation. In this case, auditory memory has evolved as a significant weakness, with visualization skills and perhaps fatigue compounding the students's academic difficulties. Weak memory skills are causing problems, but it has not been determined if that has been linked to the auditory and visualization problems.

There still are several questions one would have for this examiner:

— Why weren't many of the subtest and total test scores reported?
— What are the results of tests of phonetic ability?
— What specific behavior was exhibited?
— In remediation, should the emphasis be more on auditory skills or memory skills for efficiency?
— What are some examples of listening and memory activities?
— Why weren't all the referral problems addressed?

Psychological Report 4

NAME: George Affect
ADDRESS:
AGE: 14–8   **DOB:** 1/13/67
SEX: M   **GRADE:** 10
TEACHER: Jamie Gonzalez
DATE OF REFERRAL: 9/19/81

PARENT: Isaac Affect
TELEPHONE:
DATE OF TEST: 10/8/81
SCHOOL: Central
REFERRED BY: teacher
EXAMINER: Steve Kovatch

REASON FOR REFERRAL:

George was referred because he is experiencing continuing academic problems in the tenth-grade curriculum. His teachers report great difficulty in the language arts areas. Reading seems to be a particular problem area.

BACKGROUND INFORMATION:

George is one of four children. He has a sister, 19, and two brothers, aged 23 and 26. Pregnancy and birth were reported as essentially normal. Mrs. Affect reported that the umbilical cord was wrapped around George's neck and she was required to have oxygen during the delivery. Birth weight was 6 lbs., 1 oz.; and developmental milestones were realized within normal limits. George was originally referred for testing in 1976. At that time his fifth grade teacher reported problems in spelling and social relationships. He was placed in a learning disability resource program for fifth and sixth grades and subsequently dropped from the learning disabled roll when his achievement tested within the normal range.

PREVIOUS TESTING:

A Stanford-Binet IQ test was administered in November 1976. George earned an

IQ of 115, placing him in the high average range of intelligence.

PRESENT TESTING:

Intelligence: WISC–R

Verbal	SS	MA	%ile	Performance	SS	MA	%ile
Information	12	17–0	75	*Picture Completion	14	17+	91
Similarities	11	15–6	63	Picture Arrangement	12	17–0	75
Arithmetic	8	11–6	25	*Block Design	14	17+	91
Vocabulary	10	14–6	50	Object Assembly	13	17+	84
Comprehension	12	17–0	75	Coding	9	13–10	37
(Digit Span)	8	11–6	25				

* Indicates significantly high

Verbal IQ 103   58th %ile   Performance IQ 117   87th %ile

Full Scale IQ 110   75th %ile

Achievement

WRAT	Grade	SS	%ile
Reading	7.6	97	42
Spelling	3.9	73	4
Arithmetic	5.6	82	12

Woodcock Reading Mastery Tests

Word Identification   45th %ile
Word Attack   21st %ile

KeyMath Diagnostic Arithmetic Test

Grade Level   5.0

Low scores were in the content area of fractions, the operations areas of addition, subtraction, multiplication, division, mental computation, and numerical reasoning, and the applications areas of missing elements and time.

Other Testing

Wepman Auditory Discrimination Test

Quotient 118

This is within the normal range.

Bender Visual Motor Gestalt Test

Developmental Age: 12+ years (Time: 3¼ minutes)

Draw a Person Test

Detroit Tests of Learning Aptitude

Verbal Ability	Score (Simple/Weighted)	MA
2. Verbal Absurdities	27	12–9
4. Verbal Opposites	39	10–3

Auditory Attentive Ability	Score (Simple/Weighted)		MA
6. Auditory Attention Span for Unrelated Words	49	259	10−0
13. Auditory Attention Span for Related Syllables	82		12−3
18. Oral Directions	13		12−3

CLINICAL OBSERVATIONS:

George was given a visual screening which showed him to be nearsighted. He stated that he was supposed to wear glasses, but didn't like to and refused to wear them after second grade. At times he was reluctant to cooperate with the examiner and tried to engage in off-task behavior such as talking about the weather, football, and other topics associated with casual conversation. At times during the testing he seemed apathetic and would occasionally slump in his chair.

TEST RESULTS:

Intelligence is in the high average range. His Performance score was higher than his Verbal score, but not significantly so. This pattern is characteristic of students who have had earlier academic difficulties. Above average scores were earned on the Performance subtests of Picture Completion and Block Design. A high average score was earned on the Object Assembly subtest. This indicates good visual discrimination skills (Picture Completion) and good ability to organize concrete objects with (Block Design) or without (Object Assembly) a visual reference model. Low average scores were earned on the Verbal subtests of Arithmetic and Digit Span, indicating possible problems in auditory attention. This could be a contributing factor in his difficulty with mentally solving arithmetic problems.

George was most proficient with tasks involving spatial concepts, using visual aids, visualizing ideas, understanding oral messages, and social intelligence. He was less successful in areas requiring auditory attention, motivation, and numerical reasoning.

Achievement scores indicate a wide range of functioning. Contrary to the referral information, George achieved in the average range in reading and was significantly below average in arithmetic. Spelling was below average, but motivation problems and poor handwriting may have adversely affected his score.

In reading, he reluctantly employed phonic skills (which is a part of the curriculum in this district) to supplement an average sight vocabulary. His phonic skills are in the low average range as shown on the Word Attack subtest of the Woodcock. On an informal measure of oral reading, he frequently lost his place and his tempo was much slower than average.

In arithmetic, George can do basic simple computations with whole numbers. He is unable to solve problems involving percentages, decimals, algebra, and fractions.

George's auditory discrimination is within the normal range. He has the capability of discriminating, say, short "i" from short "e."

Perceptual-motor skills were assessed through performance on the Bender-Gestalt and Draw-a-Person tests. Bender performance indicates a strong short-term visual memory. He was able to quickly reproduce seven of the nine figures during immediate recall. His human figure drawing was described as a boy of unknown age who wasn't doing anything. It was immature and the head was drawn without hair or eyes. This drawing was similar to that expected of a 12-year old. While these tests do not indicate any significant delay in perceptual-motor development, high average or above average scores on the WISC–R subtests of Information, Picture Completion, Picture Arrangement, Block Design, and Object Assembly lead one to suspect problems with motivation. Observations noted included a lack of effort, impulsiveness, a tendency to act out, and a poor self-concept.

Results of the Detroit Test of Learning Aptitude confirm problems in auditory skills. George seemed to rely on contextual clues and his visual strengths to get through the auditory subtests.

SUMMARY AND DIAGNOSIS

George was referred primarily because he has reading problems. He is functioning in the average range of intelligence and has the potential to succeed in the normal school curriculum. His Verbal IQ is below his Performance IQ. This profile is not unusual for an individual with problems in learning. He is functioning significantly below average in the areas of spelling and arithmetic and at the low average level in his ability to employ phonics as a word attack skill. Depressed achievement scores may be attributed in part to poor auditory skills. Poor motivation, poor self-concept, and his refusal to wear glasses contribute to the poor academic progress.

In reading, he tested in the average range. His inability to keep his place and a slow oral reading rate, however, are probably causing some comprehension problems. Strengths were noted in visual-motor skills. Even in tasks involving auditory abilities, he tried to rely on visual skills and contextual clues for solutions.

Based on these data, George qualifies for learning disability services.

RECOMMENDATIONS

1. George is hindered by his refusal to wear his glasses. The most obvious solution is to get an opthamalogical exam and follow the resulting recommendations, including the wearing of prescription lenses if advised. Until this takes place, George should be seated closely enough to the board or screen so that he can comfortably read the material presented.

2. In arithmetic, George is having the most difficulty with the more abstract requirements. He probably needs to see and handle directly what he is to learn. Concrete manipulatives would help at first and problems should be placed in a functional context. George should learn that problems should be attacked in a systematic manner through use of algorithms.

3. It may help to cue him by saying, "George, listen!" before giving directions.

4. George should be encouraged to repeat auditory information to himself. This is a rehearsal strategy. At first, he may have to re-state directions which the teacher has just given orally.

5. In language arts areas, several recommendations can be made. George might benefit from a multimodal approach to spelling, such as the Fernald technique. In reading, a choral reading approach should improve his rate and increase his fluidity and confidence. Perhaps some visual tracking exercises should be tried. At the same time, strategies for gaining meaning from the printed page should be taught. George has demonstrated strengths in his ability to use contextual clues.

   Although his auditory skills are weak, George relies a great deal on his phonic skills. He has adequate auditory discrimination skills. It cannot be assumed that his sound-symbol correspondence skills are adequate. This should be checked. Sound blending skills should be taught, perhaps through use of the Hegge, Kirk, and Kirk drills.

Posture in handwriting is poor and should be improved. George uses an incorrect grip, is tense during writing, and positions his paper incorrectly. He should be encouraged to pull his downward strokes in a direction parallel to his paper and rest the tips of the last two fingers on the paper. This should give him some immediate success and provide further encouragement for future efforts. Use of a commercial program such as that published by Zaner-Bloser or Scott-Foresman would probably be beneficial. George should be encouraged to learn better penmanship on his own.

6. George would probably benefit from some form of program in which he could receive immediate feedback. He also needs to learn that the responsibility for his learning lies within himself.

It is not too late to employ basic remediation strategies with George. In the event that this fails, the recommendation would then be to teach him how to use a calculator and typewriter and also hope that he will maintain enough interest in reading at least to want to read the newspaper or to do some leisure reading.

This report fulfills the requirements set forth in the beginning of this chapter. From it a teacher who has general knowledge of the statistics of testing should be able to plan some informal assessment strategies for and provide a learning atmosphere geared toward the needs of George. It would help the teacher if the actual test protocols (forms, records, blanks, answer sheets) were available for inspection.

Of the four reports presented, a teacher is most likely to deal with those like that of Audri, the third report presented. To understand this fully, it is necessary to do some interpretation. This process will be greatly facilitated if a teacher has an understanding of the meaning of test statistics. First, however, it might be in order to review the purposes of testing and its relationship to teaching. This will be done in Chapter 2 and throughout the remainder of this book.

REFERENCES

Ann Arbor tracking program. 1980. Naples, Florida: Ann Arbor Publishers.

Baker, H. J., and Leland, B. 1967. *Detroit tests of learning aptitude,* rev. ed. Indianapolis: Bobbs-Merrill.

Barbe, W., Lucas, H., Hackney, C., and McAllister, C. 1979. *Creative growth with handwriting,* 2nd ed. Columbus, Ohio: Zaner-Bloser.

Bender, L. 1968. *A visual-motor gestalt test and its clinical use.* New York: American Orthopsychiatric Association Research Monograph no. 3.

Connolly, A. J., Nachtman, W., and Pritchett, E. M. 1970. *KeyMath diagnostic arithmetic test.* Circle Pines, Minnesota: American Guidance Service.

Fernald, G. 1943. *Remedial techniques in basic school subjects.* New York: McGraw-Hill.

Hegge, T., Kirk, S., and Kirk, W. 1940/1965. *Remedial reading drills.* Ann Arbor, Michigan: George Wahr Publishing.

Jastak, J. F., and Jastak, S. R. 1978. *Wide range achievement test.* Wilmington, Delaware: Jastak Associates.

Kirk, S. A., McCarthy, J. J., and Kirk, W. D. 1968. *The Illinois test of psycholinguistic abilities,* rev. ed. Urbana, Illinois: University of Illinois Press.

Kirk, W. 1975. *A format for psychologial reports.* Tucson, Arizona: Mimeographed copy, University of Arizona.

Otis, A. S., and Lennon, R. T. 1967. *Otis-Lennon mental ability test.* New York: Harcourt, Brace, and World.

Silvaroli, N. J. 1976. *Classroom reading inventory,* 3rd ed. Dubuque, Iowa: William C. Brown.

Slosson, R. L. 1973. *Slosson intelligence test for children and adults.* East Aurora, New York: Slosson Educational Publications.

Terman, L. M., and Merrill, M. A. 1973. *Stanford-Binet intelligence scale: 1972 norms ed.* Boston: Houghton-Mifflin.

Thurber, D. N. 1978. *D'Nealian handwriting.* Glenview, Illinois: Scott, Foresman.

Urban, W. 1963. *Draw-a-person.* Los Angeles: Western Psychological Services.

Wechsler, D. 1974. *Wechsler intelligence scale for children—revised.* New York: Psychological Corporation.

Wepman, J. 1958. *Auditory discrimination test.* Chicago: Language Research Associates.

Woodcock, R. W. 1972. *Woodcock reading mastery tests.* Circle Pines, Minnesota: American Guidance Service.

CHAPTER 2

THE MYSTERIES OF TESTING

Humans are generally imbued with insatiable curiosity. This trait has led to the exploration of the planet and beyond, the world too small to see, and the intricacies of human behavior. The variability of human performance has fascinated many people to the point of obsession. Perhaps the complexity of human response is the motivator; perhaps the desire for order leads to the attempts to match human aptitude, interests, and functioning with specific curricula and careers. In any event, the desire to observe, examine, classify, explain, exploit, expedite, and know has helped to shape a world in which testing plays a major role.

Testing to Harm

A popular statement among teachers today is that testing may be detrimental to children's self-concepts. The rationale follows these steps:

1. Test items are too difficult.
2. Children who take tests experience failure.
3. Failure leads to frustration, generalized to a hatred of school and self.
4. Lower school achievement results.
5. Testing, therefore, is counterproductive because it leads to lower achievement.

A second problem with testing involves its use in making placement decisions. It has been found that many children were inappropriately placed in classes for the handicapped primarily on the basis of test scores. Inappropriate placement may lead to lowered expectations and, hence, lower achievement. This could result in lowered career aspirations and less success in occupational pursuits. It has also been argued that the stigma associated with bearing the label of being handicapped further lowers self-concept. Handicapped children often have the added burden of being taunted and baited by their peers who are thought to be "normal."

A third criticism of testing is that it does not yield enough practical information. Many feel that the time and resources consumed in the testing process do not justify the paucity of useful classroom suggestions generated. It is just not good enough to spend a considerable amount of resources to conclude that a child functions at a 3.2 grade level in reading.

These arguments have been persuasive to the point that safeguards have been mandated through legislation, litigation, and regulation. Testing must now be performed in a manner which safeguards the rights of students. But this may not be enough in light of the seriousness of the effects of testing. Perhaps educators should reconsider the whole realm of psychoeducational testing with a view toward elimination or severe curtailment of formal, standardized testing with school children. If testing is counterproductive or if insufficient information is gained from testing, then why continue it?

Why Test?

Controversy continues to surround the role of testing in education. As instruments, tests can be seriously flawed. Test items reflecting racial, cultural, or gender bias have been reported. Some experts even advocate that formal testing be discontinued as a component of the special education placement process. Others believe that the amount of useful information obtained justifies the use of tests.

Testing as a process also is receiving a great deal of scrutiny. Much of the distrust with testing may not necessarily lie with the instruments or the concepts inherent in psychoeducational testing, but with the way in which test instruments are used. Batteries of tests given to all as screening devices allow large amounts of data to be collected, but may also create an artificial need for additional testers.

Often, tests are expected to do more than they were designed to do. Screening tests have been used to diagnose disabilities, intelligence tests have been used to determine academic achievement or diagnose learning or social problems, and tests designed for use with primary aged children have been used in secondary situations. This list is by no means exhaustive. To gain useful information, tests must be used within the scope of their design.

While many abuses have been associated with psychoeducational testing, it is probably unfair to say that testing inherently leads to lower achievement, questionable to say that labels lead to lower achievement, and quite proper to expect more than a grade-level score to result from formal testing.

There is a fundamental difference between testing and teaching. In testing, the examiner wishes to find out what a child does and does not know at a given point in time. With this information, one hopes that instruction for an individual or group may be accomplished in a more efficient manner. To discover what a child can and cannot do, it is necessary to have a relatively large number of items which may range from easy to difficult. For purposes of precision, a test must have items that a child is not expected to answer correctly. Only in this manner can a meaningful profile or picture of how a child functions be obtained. Formal or standardized tests are used to compare a child with her peers. With this information, the competent examiner is able to ascertain present performance and predict future performance so that the most ideal educational programming can be supplied to the child.

In teaching, the educator is interested in effecting positive behavioral change and will try to facilitate correct responses on the part of students. If students understand this distinction, testing need be only transitorily frustrating, if frustrating at all. A dose of success afterwards in the teaching process is usually quite beneficial. Both testing and teaching are integral parts of the educational process, but each has a different purpose.

Inappropriate placement as the result of testing is one of the travesties of education. It should be every educator's ethical responsibility to see that the incidences of mislabeling are reduced. This can be done by careful monitoring of each child's progress in school. The implication is that salaried school personnel *should* know the fundamentals of testing. Relatively new evidence indicates that the concept of "self-fulfilling prophecy" may have been overstated. Perhaps a certain comfort can be taken in the adage that children learn in spite of teachers' efforts. The effects of wrongful placement can be devastating, nevertheless.

There is also a difference in testing for a purpose and testing to see whether or not "anything shows up." Screening is done routinely to catch potential difficulties. Beyond that, each test given should be administered for a specific purpose, or else much duplication of effort and wasted time can result. This is why the person who writes referrals must make these as succinct as possible. If everyone in the process understands what is expected and why, the tester can quickly zero-in on the problem or problems of each child and report, in very specific terms, the child's level of functioning. This is the only way a child can be most efficiently served by the educational system.

Parents have heard the adage that, if a child is given a hammer, the whole world needs pounding. Applied to testing, if an examiner is given a test battery, every child needs that battery. Some examiners are test-happy. They seem to have forgotten that a test should not be given until a specific reason for giving it has been stated. Those who test for the sake of testing sometimes give the impression that numbers or statistics, rather than helping children to learn, are the *sine qua non* of the testing process. Unfortunately in many places, those who test do not necessarily have to have the benefit of teaching experience or the opportunity to participate in the real world of the classroom. Testing is a part of the instructional process and as such, should have as its outcome practical recommendations for teaching. *It must never be forgotten that the overall purpose of testing is to improve instruction.*

Besides placement, testing serves a number of purposes. It is possible to list eight reasons for testing.

1. To determine the child who is exceptional. This child is either not coping as a result of a handicap or is in need of an accelerated program to work to potential. Screening and classification are included here. A comprehensive assessment has been mandated in the areas of intelligence, achievement, adaptive behavior, and—in some cases—psycholinguistic functioning.
2. To check the efficacy of curriculum, methods, and materials. Outcomes of instruction are measured so that better educational programming can be delivered. The evaluation of commercial programs should always include a scrutiny of field test data.
3. To judge pupil progress. This is necessary for a number of reasons, including grouping for subjects, assigning students to classes based upon a match between student learning and instructor teaching styles, grading, and promotion.
4. To guide and counsel. Many graduates have no idea of what they want to do in life. In fact, many have not even been able to narrow their options to one or two of the fifteen occupational clusters as described by the United States Office of Education (1971). A number of tests can help in the process of matching aptitudes, interests, and capabilities to available career areas.
5. To make administrative decisions. Testing can be an aid to educational policy-making in such areas as length of school day, age at which school is started, and whether social promotions should or should not be granted.
6. To select and retain staff. This is a very controversial area. So many variables are involved in building an effective educational program that it is difficult to justify basing decisions on the limited amount of data a test will generate.
7. To have a common language for communication. When one says that a child is "doing well," it may be interpreted differently by others. A much more precise way to communicate that observation is to say that the child earned a grade score of 3.2 in arithmetic, or scored at the 85th percentile, or gained the 90-percent criterion level in third-grade arithmetic.
8. To increase the efficiency of learning. Information gained from testing can be interpreted to yield better curricula and methods. This knowledge can often take five to ten years to reach the classroom in usable form. The amount of research being performed suggests that exciting educational activities will continue to be made available to teachers.

Kinds of Tests

Two types of tests are used to help school-age children. Norm-referenced tests are used to compare a child with other children. These are also called formal or standardized tests and are discussed in Chapter 10.

Criterion-referenced tests are used to demonstrate mastery of a task or tasks. Here, a performance level or criterion level is set, such as 90 percent, and the student must attain that level to demonstrate competence. Most criterion-referenced tests are teacher-made and may be nothing more than a page taken from a child's workbook. Test publishers have in recent years made available commercially prepared criterion-referenced instruments. Often, these are hybrids; others have not reported normed data. Criterion-referenced tests are discussed in Chapters 3 and 13.

School Uses of Tests

Norm-referenced and criterion-referenced tests are used in schools in three areas: aptitude, achievement, and personality. Aptitude testing is used to predict future performance in some activity or to judge the ability to learn new tasks. IQ testing is the most prevalent type of aptitude measurement, and virtually all testing in this area is of the norm-referenced type. Placement in special education depends heavily on the results obtained through IQ testing.

Achievement testing is used to determine what a child has learned. Reading achievement is divided into vocabulary (the meaning of words) and comprehension (the meaning of passages). In some cases, oral reading is checked for a number of factors. A great deal of reading instruments are available. Many informal reading measures are devised by teachers daily. A good discussion of this may be found in the text by Ekwall (1981).

Another major section of achievement testing is in language. Usage (the mechanics of language—punctuation, capitalization, tense, etc.), expression (conciseness, flow, precision, correctness, unity, cohesiveness, and effectiveness), and spelling may be checked. Many workbooks and other commercial programs are available for measurement and instruction in this area.

The third major section of achievement testing is in arithmetic. A number of organizational schema are used. The *KeyMath*, for example, is broken down into the areas of content (numeration, fractions, and geometry and symbols), operations (addition, subtraction, multiplication, division, mental computation, and numerical reasoning), and applications (word problems, missing elements, money, measurement, and time). Informal testing procedures in this area are covered in a number of texts, including one by Ashlock (1972).

Finally, achievement testing may include study skills, although this is less likely. Outlining skills, library skills, and the ability to interpret maps, graphs, and tables comprise the components of this section.

Special education operates on a failure model. A student generally must demonstrate failure to the point of falling significantly behind his classmates before being labeled handicapped and placed in a special education setting for help. Achievement testing is used to confirm academic failure.

Personality testing is the third type of norm-referenced and criterion-referenced testing used in schools. In comparison with aptitude and achievement measures, personality testing is used to a very small extent. Included here are measures of adjustment, attitude, and interest. Much more interest has been shown in this area recently because poor adaptive behavior, a subset of adjustment, is now an element which must be shown for the diagnosis of mental retardation. Another factor in the increasing interest in personality testing has to do with the movement toward the infusion of career education into the curricula at all grade levels. This interest should spur test makers to develop greatly improved tests in this area.

Each test has been designed for a specific purpose. It is up to those who use tests to make sure that each test is used appropriately. Before any test is given, the examiner should have in mind a goal that the test will help achieve. The purpose of testing is to help children achieve at the highest possible level. No other purpose supercedes this. The mystery of testing is that not enough people seem to follow this dictum.

REFERENCES

Anastasi, A. 1976. *Psychological testing,* 4th ed. New York: Macmillan.

Ashlock, R. B. 1972. *Error patterns in computation.* Columbus, Ohio: Charles E. Merrill.

Connolly, A. J., Nachtman, W., and Pritchett, E. M. 1970. *KeyMath diagnostic arithmetic test.* Circle Pines, Minnesota: American Guidance Service.

Ekwall, E. E. 1981. *Locating and correcting reading difficulties,* 3rd ed. Columbus, Ohio: Charles E. Merrill.

Green, J. A. 1970. *Introduction to measurement and evaluation.* New York: Dodd, Mead.

Gronlund, N. E. 1971. *Measurement and evaluation in teaching,* 2nd ed. New York: Macmillan.

Kass, C. E. 1976. Testing versus teaching. Personal communication.

Noether, G. 1971. *Introduction to statistics: a fresh approach.* Boston: Houghton-Mifflin.

Noll, V. H., and Scannell, D. P. 1972. *Introduction to educational measurement,* 3rd ed. Boston: Houghton-Mifflin.

Salvia, J., and Ysseldyke, J. E. 1981. *Assessment in special and remedial education,* 2nd ed. Boston: Houghton-Mifflin.

United States Office of Education. 1971. *Career education.* Washington, D.C.: Government Printing Office.

Wallace, G., and Larsen, S. A. 1978. *Educational assessment of learning problems.* Boston: Allyn and Bacon.

CHAPTER 3

AN OVERVIEW OF STATISTICS

The numbers obtained through testing often don't seem to have any basis in reality. This is because testing is based on techniques not usually understood by those who should be their consumers, the teachers. Preservice and inservice training is most often concerned with teaching tools other than test interpretation. Many people believe that testing is *supposed* to be mysterious. In fact, many teachers feel that, once the psychoeducational testing of a child is completed, the gobbledegook can be filed away so that the real work can be started. Some school systems encourage this attitude by not giving teachers access to psychoeducational test data or by not requiring that psychological reports be written in language that teachers can understand.

Besides having to deal with mysterious numbers, teachers have difficulty relating the numerical information, once digested, to the conclusions and recommendations stated in evaluation reports. This is because the theoretical orientation of the report writer is not generally stated in the report. Relating numbers to problems involves some discussion of the relationship between child development and numbers. Child development is beyond the scope of this book. Numbers are used in many ways. The particular numbers of interest here are called statistics.

Statistics and Measurement

Statistics, as a term, has been defined in many ways, but generally can be thought of as belonging to one of three concepts.

1. Statistics are numbers which can be used to summarize, analyze, or evaluate a body of information.
2. Statistics is a separate subject like penmanship, reading, or chemistry. It can be thought of as a body of methods for making wise choices in the face of uncertainty.
3. Statistics are numbers associated with a sample group. A sample group is a subset or part of the whole group or population.

Once we get past the definition stage, the confusion is lessened because the operations performed through statistical techniques are much less subject to dispute. Statistical operations can be applied to numbers obtained by measurement. Measurement may be thought of as the gathering of objective data (i.e., numbers). Testing is a part of measurement. Also included in psychoeducational measurement are rating scales, checklists, inventories, and score cards. Measurement, then, is the description of an object or concept through numbers.

These numbers may be expressed as continuous or discrete measures. Examples of continuous measures include height, weight, length, width, IQ, temperature, and time. It is assumed that continuous measures can only be approximated. This is because the mathematical construct involved states that, between any two points on a measuring device, there are an infinite number of points. Therefore, measuring devices such as tests or rulers or scales can never be completely accurate, but only approximate. The better the measuring device, the more accurate the measurement, but it is assumed that, because of the infinite distance between two points, complete accuracy is not possible. This is why, for example, differences of several IQ points are not considered meaningful, and why people asked to measure objects such as the top of a desk obtain different figures.

Discrete measures are whole units or counters. These measures are used to count events which either happen or do not happen. The number of times a pigeon depresses a lever is an example of a discrete datum.

Measurement and Objectives

People who don't have a clear understanding of the differences between continuous and discrete measures may have trouble when they try to write educational objectives. An objective expressed in discrete units of evaluation is much easier to write and use than continuous units. The following objective is an example: "Given a worksheet with fifty one-digit plus one-digit problems, John will write the answers with no less than forty-five of fifty (90 percent) correct." Here it is easy to mark each problem as correct or incorrect and count the correct responses.

The evaluation of a child's competence when the objective is written in terms of continuous data is much more difficult. Consider the following objective: "Upon command, the student will write in cursive the sentence, 'Jack and Jill went up the hill,' with proper letter size, slant, and spacing."

Is the following response proper?

Jacks and Jills went ups the hill

Is this response proper?

Jack and Jill went up the hill

There is no way to count the correct responses and tabulate these as a percentage of the whole, because there are an infinite number of mistakes a child could make. At any point in the sentence, the child could deviate from the correct response.

The question becomes one of how much deviation will be tolerated so that the response still remains within the boundaries of correctness. With continuous data such as this, a degree of subjectivity is introduced. Two people looking at the written sentences may differ over the correctness of the size, slant, and spacing of the letters unless a specific, external standard of comparison exists.

Because discrete evaluation is the easier of the two to perform, the objective writer would do well to make continuous data discrete. Where this is not possible, the writer should at least try to decrease the subjectivity involved in the judgment of student response. The following objective, although unwieldly, is written in more objective terms: "Upon command, the fourth-grade student will write on lined paper the sentence in cursive, 'Jack and Jill went up the hill,' with no ascender above the midline except where appropriate or above the top line, and no descender below the baseline or descender line as appropriate, with each vertical stroke no more than 20 degrees to the left of perpendicular or 40 degrees to the right of perpendicular, no more than four letters per inch nor less than three per inch, and between one-quarter and three-eighths inches between words."

To do this for each objective in which continuous data is involved is absurd in terms of effort expended. Fortunately, others have devised systems of evaluation which work well, although it may be necessary to give up some objectivity. This objective could be written: "Upon command, the student will write in cursive the sentence, 'Jack and Jill went up the hill,' approximating the Zaner-Bloser model for the average fourth-grade student four out of five times attempted."

Statistical techniques may be applied to both continuous and discrete data. This book emphasizes the understanding of standardized testing and the statistics applied in that testing. It is assumed that the measurement of grade levels, age levels, IQ, and the like, involves the collection of continuous data and its manipulation through the techniques associated with descriptive statistics. Statistics are divided into two major categories. These are descriptive and inferential.

Categories of Statistics and Scales

Descriptive statistics are used to describe or summarize data. They may be used for characterizations of the individuals or groups being observed. Inferential statistics are the other major category of statistics. The person who employs inferential statistics is trying to make generalizations beyond the data at hand, estimate unknown values, or evaluate differences among groups.

Numbers used for statistical purposes fall into one of four categories or scales. These are: nominal, ordinal, interval, and ratio. The nominal scale is a numerical label or a measure of identity. Numbers are used to place objects or people into categories. Examples would include automobile or appliance-model numbers, the Dewey Decimal Classification System for libraries, and class intervals in a frequency distribution. One statistic, the mode (described in Chapter 4), is most frequently used with nominal data. In special cases, two sets of nominal data may be compared. This relationahip is expressed as a phi (ϕ) coefficient or tetrachoric correlation coefficient, depending on the nature of the data. Nominal data relationships are rarely used in psychoeducational testing and will not be discussed in this book.

The ordinal scale is associated with data which can be ranked. It is a measure of the relative quality or quantity of a given trait which objects possess. The rankings have little value outside a specific group. Beauty and subjective judgment are examples of traits which may be ranked, but it is assumed that the symbols used don't show the amount of difference between the adjacent ranks. Because of this, it is not possible to add, subtract, multiply, or divide ranked data. Statistics which may be applied to ordinal data include the mode (see Chapter 4), median (Chapter 4), range (Chapter 5), semi-interquartile range (Chapter 6), and percentile (Chapter 7). When two sets of ordinal data are compared, the relationship is expressed as a Spearman rank-order (r_s or ρ [rho]) correlation coefficient or as a Kendall's τ (tau) coefficient. Ordinal data relationships are rarely used in psychoeducational testing and will not be covered in this book.

The interval scale has equal units. Here the difference between, say, 1163 and 1164 is the same as the difference between 56 and 57. Zero is established as a point on this scale, but it is not absolute and does not denote the absence of the trait or quality being measured. Examples of interval scales include IQ scores and the Centigrade and Farenheit thermometers. Interval data may be added, subtracted, multiplied, and divided. Statistical operations which may be applied to interval data include all those used with ordinal data plus the mean or average (Chapter 4), standard deviation (Chapter 6), Pearson product-moment correlation or r (Chapter 8), and two techniques not covered in this text—t-tests and F-tests. Both are most often used to compare the means of two groups. Neither is generally applied in psychoeducational testing.

The ratio scale is similar to the interval scale except that zero in this scale is absolute. Here, zero indicates complete absence of the trait or quality being meausred. Examples include the Kelvin thermometer, chronological age of people, and many of the measurement scales used in educational and psychological testing (e.g., achievement). All mathematical calculations may be performed with ratio data.

In education and psychology, it is most convenient to collect either interval or ratio data for testing purposes. This is because more kinds of statistical techniques can be applied to this data and consequently, more information can be apprehended. Both the interval and ratio scales assume continuous measurement.

In psychoeducational testing, the teacher is most interested in obtaining a description of a child's current level of functioning. Knowledge of descriptive techniques is essential for greatest efficiency in instructional planning. The next seven chapters will present descriptive statistical procedures in some detail as a prerequisite to the use of tests as instructional tools.

REFERENCES

Anderson, T. R., and Zelditch, M. 1968. *A basic course in statistics,* 2nd ed. New York: Holt, Rinehart, and Winston.

Chase, C. I. 1967. *Elementary statistical procedures.* New York: McGraw-Hill.

Downie, N. M., and Heath, R. W. 1970. *Basic statistical methods,* 3rd ed. New York: Harper and Row.

Green, J. A. 1970. *Introduction to measurement and evaluation.* New York: Dodd, Mead.

Gronlund, N. E. 1971. *Measurement and evaluation in teaching,* 2nd ed. New York: Macmillan.

Hickman, E. P., and Hilton, J. G. 1971. *Probability and statistical analysis.* Scranton, Pennsylvania: Intext.

Noll, V. H., and Scannell, D. P. 1972. *Introduction to educational measurement,* 3rd ed. Boston: Houghton-Mifflin.

Noether, G. 1971. *Introduction to statistics: a fresh approach.* Boston: Houghton-Mifflin.

Schmidt, M. 1975. *Understanding and using statistics: basic concepts.* Lexington, Massachusetts: D. C. Heath.

Wallis, W., and Roberts, H. 1965. *The nature of statistics.* New York: Free Press.

CHAPTER 4

CENTRAL TENDENCY

To understand statistics, some basic techniques must be mastered. Many authors feel that knowledge of measures of central tendency or averages is the point of departure into statisticsland. An average is a typical value or most likely value in a set of scores. It is a number used to summarize a set of scores and is a convenient one-number indicator of a trend in a set of scores. There is great value placed upon knowing how close to or distant from average a score falls. Comparison of averages is a common statistical technique. The three most common averages or measures of central tendency are the mean, the median, and the mode.

Mean

The mean may be used with interval and ratio scales of measurement. It is depicted as M or $\overline{X}$ and is the most commonly used average because it lends itself most easily to statistical testing. To find the mean, take the sum of a group of scores (ΣX) and divide by the total number of scores (n). In the following group of scores, 36, 44, 45, 53, 54, 55, 55, 58, the calculation would be as follows:

$$\overline{X} = \frac{\Sigma X}{n}$$

$$\Sigma X = 36 + 44 + 45 + 53 + 54 + 55 + 55 + 58 = 400$$

$$n = 8$$

$$\overline{X} = \frac{400}{8} = 50$$

Picture this concept as a balance beam with the balance point or fulcrum as the mean or arithmetic average.

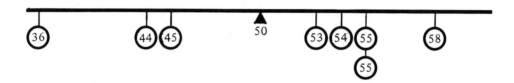

Each score has the same weight. The beam balances because the sums of the distances from the mean on each side (of the mean) are equal. In the illustration, the left side distances are $14 + 6 + 5$, or 25, and the right side distances are $3 + 4 + 5 + 5 + 8$, or 25. Try this procedure with the following set of scores: 87, 90, 108, 110, 110.

Because the numbers in the above examples lie within a relatively narrow range, the mean gives an accurate picture of the average score. If there is a large cluster of scores in a relatively narrow range and a few scores at an extreme distance, however, the mean may yield a distorted summary of the set of scores. For example, the set of scores 10, 11, 11, 12, 13, 13, 15, 15, 15, 16, 17, 17, 17, 17, 18, 21, 25, 89, 90, 90 yields a mean of 26.

$$\overline{X} = \frac{\Sigma X}{n} = \frac{520}{20} = 26$$

In view of the fact that most of the scores lie between 10 and 17, this average seems to color the representation of reality. In a case like this, another average might be taken to yield a more complete picture. This second average is the median.

Median

The median may be used with ordinal, interval, and ratio scales of measurement. It is the middle score in a set of scores. Fifty percent of the scores lie above and 50 percent of the scores lie below the median. Two symbols used to indicate the median are Mdn and P_{50}. Fewer computations can be performed with the median than the mean; consequently, the median is used much less often. The median may be referred to as the counting average or average of position; as such, the impact of a few extreme scores upon the total set of scores is lessened. When both the mean and median are reported, a more complete picture of the set of scores is gained. In the case of an odd number of scores, the median is the middle score. It is ordinarily found by ordering the scores from lowest to highest and counting until the middle score is found.

For example, in the set 1, 2, 4, 6, 8, 9, 10, the median is 6. Three scores lie to the right of 6, and three scores lie to the left. In the following example 10, 11, 11, 12, 13, 13, 15, 15, 15, 16, 17, 17, 17, 17, 18, 21, 25, 89, 90, 90, there is no middle score. Here the median would lie exactly between the two scores closest to the middle. The calculation would be:

$$Mdn = \frac{16 + 17}{2} = 16.5.$$

There are 10 scores below 16.5 and 10 scores above 16.5. Remember that the mean was 26 for this set of scores. By computing both averages, the reader has an indication that the set of scores is distorted and that perhaps a truer average of the majority of scores is 16.5.

The following is a list of sets of scores for practice in finding the mean and median.

1. 14, 26, 31, 35, 35, 36, 39, 47. $\Sigma = 260$ $\overline{X} = 32.5$ $P_{50} = 35$

2. 87, 91, 92, 95, 96, 96, 99, 101, 105, 110, 113, 114, 118, 118, 119.
    $\Sigma = 1554$ $\overline{X} = 103.6$ $P_{50} = 101$

3. 26, 31, 35, 36, 47, 89, 97, 98, 99, 102, 103, 104, 104, 109, 120.
    $\Sigma = 1200$ $\overline{X} = 80$ $P_{50} = 98$

4. 8, 8, 8, 8, 8, 10, 10, 10, 11, 13, 14, 36, 46, 46, 46, 46, 48, 48, 49, 69.
    $\Sigma = 542$ $\overline{X} = 27$ $P_{50} = 13.5$

Mode

The mode may be used with nominal, ordinal, interval, and ratio scales of measurement. Because it is the most frequent or popular score, no calculations are needed. The mode is found by inspecting the list of scores for the score which appears most often. In the following set of scores, 1, 2, 2, 2, 3, 4, 4, 4, 5, 5, 6, 6, 6, 6, 6, 6, 6, 8, 9, 9, the mode is 6. Compare that value to the mean,

$$\overline{X} = \frac{\Sigma X}{n} = \frac{100}{20} = 5$$

and the median,

$$Mdn = \frac{5+6}{2} = 5.5.$$

Here each measure of central tendency gives an accurate picture of the trend of scores.

Although the mode is rarely used, in some cases it is important as an indicator of the majority, and its advantage is that there is no influence by a few extreme scores or atypical middle scores. In the following set of scores, 9, 9, 10, 10, 11, 11, 11, 11, 12, 12, 12, 13, 13, 13, 14, 14, 35, 40, 45, 55,

$$\overline{X} = \frac{360}{20} = 18$$

and is influenced by the four relatively extreme scores of 35, 40, 45, and 55. The median is

$$Mdn = \frac{12+12}{2} = 12$$

and seems quite representative of the trend of scores, most of which lie between 9 and 14. The mode is 11 and also is representative of the trend of scores.

Consider the following set of scores: 21, 55, 27, 59, 27, 74, 27, 27, 77, 28, 78, 31, 32, 78, 78, 38, 78, 42, 81, 82. The mean is

$$\overline{X} = \frac{1040}{20} = 52$$

and the median is

$$Mdn = \frac{45+53}{2} = 49.$$

If this group of scores represents the results of a test of 100 sounds and blends, the teacher might conclude that the students needed more group drill. Upon closer inspection, a different conclusion would be reached. The mode for this set of scores occurs at two places—27 and 78. This set of scores is said to be bimodal. With this information the teacher can more easily see that for instructional purposes, two groups have emerged. Those who scored around 27 need either a great deal of instruction or a different method than phonics. Those who scored around 78 need some practice and a bit more instruction for mastery.

Problems

The following examples are provided for practice. Compute the mean, median, and mode, and draw conclusions for instruction.

1. Addition facts—50 problems in 2 minutes. Scores of the twenty students taking the addition facts test: 45, 47, 47, 47, 47, 47, 47, 48, 48, 48, 48, 48, 48, 48, 49, 49, 49, 50, 50, 50.
2. Test—writing the names of all of the presidents of the United States from memory. Scores of the twenty students taking the test: 11, 14, 15, 16, 16, 28, 28, 28, 28, 28, 28, 35, 35, 36, 36, 37, 37, 37, 38, 38.
3. Reading aloud the Dolch list of 220 words. Scores of the twenty students taking the reading test: 10, 40, 41, 43, 80, 91, 103, 104, 104, 151, 153, 154, 159, 171, 175, 176, 183, 197, 198, 199.
4. Solving ten story problems. Scores of the fifteen students taking the test: 0, 0, 0, 0, 0, 0, 1, 1, 1, 1, 2, 2, 2, 2, 3.

Answers

1. $\bar{X}$ = 48. Mdn = 48. Mode = 48. Conclusion: addition facts have been mastered. The whole class is ready to go on to the next objective.
2. $\bar{X}$ = 28.45. Mdn = 28. Mode = 28. Conclusion: measures of central tendency are deceiving because about half of the class is doing quite well, about a third need more practice, and the rest seem to be lost at this point.
3. $\bar{X}$ = 126.6. Mdn = 152. Mode = 104. Conclusion: measures of central tendency indicate that a very heterogeneous group exists. The scores are so spread out that no trend is evident.
4. $\bar{X}$ = 1. Mdn = 1. Mode = 0. Conclusion: the whole class needs instruction. Because the scores are so uniformly low, prerequisite skills should be checked.

REFERENCES

Miller, D. M. 1972. *Interpreting test scores.* New York: Wiley.
Schmidt, M. 1975. *Understanding and using statistics: basic concepts.* Lexington, Massachusetts: D. C. Heath.

CHAPTER 5

DISTRIBUTION

A distribution is a picture or summary of a group or set of scores. It is a convenient way of presenting trends in data and may take the form of a table or graph.

Tables

In tablular form, the data in the distribution are usually ordered in some logical way, such as least to greatest. When each datum is placed in the table, the result is a list. The following is an example of a list.

Name	IQ Score	Name	IQ Score	Name	IQ Score
Bob	78	Jo	85	Joan	94
Susie	78	Jason	85	Norman	94
John	78	Rhonda	85	Karen	94
Jim	80	Ellen	85	Cathy	96
Fred	81	George	85	Floyd	96
Roy	81	Byron	85	Bryan	99
Matt	83	Tim	92	Cindy	99
Mark	84	Mary	92	Don	99
Joe	84	Steve	94	Beth	101
Marge	85	Jack	94	Ann	103

This type of table is generally not used to summarize a group of scores because of the great amount of space it takes and because there is some difficulty in interpreting a relatively unorganized mass of data. A frequency distribution is more commonly used. Scores are listed once with the number of times each score was earned. The following is an example.

IQ Score	Frequency	IQ Score	Frequency
78	3	92	2
80	1	94	5
81	2	96	2
83	1	99	3
84	2	101	1
85	7	103	1

People seem to have trouble grasping a mass of numbers. It is easier to understand a more condensed summary. As seen in the last chapter, the mean, median, and mode may not by themselves give enough information. These summary numbers give some indication of trends, but many people feel they need to see more. A more condensed table may be used in which scores are clustered, as in the following example.

IQ Scores	Frequency
70–79	3
80–84	6
85–89	7
90–94	7
95–99	5
100–104	2

Graphs

Probably the most quickly grasped and easily understood summary of numbers occurs in charted form. Two of the most commonly used charts or graphs are the frequency polygon and the histogram.

The frequency polygon is usually set up as an arithmetic chart in which the ordinate (vertical line) represents the frequency or number of occurrences or percentages of a score and the abscissa (horizontal line) represents all possible scores or a time framework. As an example, IQ scores cited above have been charted as a frequency polygon.

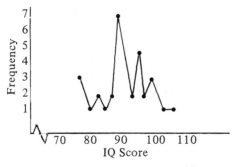

Progress of an individual may also be charted in this manner. Following is an example of a table and a graph of a student's attempt to achieve mastery in using the proper verb tense by filling in the blanks of several sentence exercises.

Day	1	2	3	4	5	6	7	8
Score	0	1	1	2	4	3	5	5

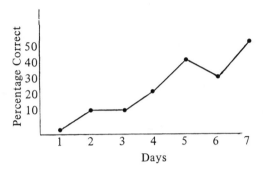

When scores are grouped, the histogram is used. As an example, the IQ scores grouped into five-point clusters earlier have been charted as a histogram.

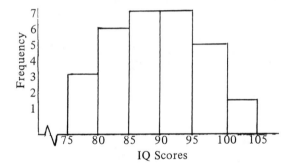

As more and more data are added to the graph, there is a tendency for the figure to approximate a normal, bell-shaped (Gaussian) curve.

The Normal Curve

Distributions are obtained by observation. The observer applies some type of measure to a characteristic such as mental ability or achievement and notes the various measurements in a systematic fashion. This is known as the empirical method. As more and more measures of a characteristic are taken, the graph of the measures begins to take on the following shape.

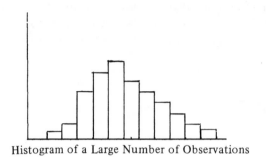

Histogram of a Large Number of Observations

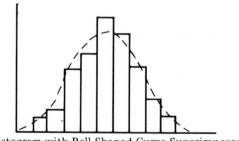

Frequency Polygon of a Large Number of Observations

By smoothing out the two graphs, bell-shaped curves emerge. Note that in this type of curve there is a large group of scores or measures clustered around the measure of central tendency, and the mean, median, and mode fall at the same point. As one goes away from the mean in either direction, the frequency of appearance of the scores or measures drops off in a regular fashion.

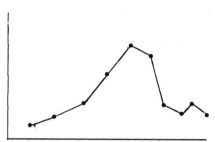

Histogram with Bell-Shaped Curve Superimposed

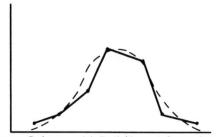

Frequency Polygon with Bell-Shaped Curve Superimposed

When the curve is defined by the formula

$$Y = \frac{\sqrt{n}}{\Sigma\,(X - \bar{X})\sqrt{2\pi}}\ e^{-\frac{X^{2}n}{2\Sigma\,(X - \bar{X})^{2}}}$$

where n = the number of scores, e = the natural log or 2.7183, and $X\,(X - X)$ = the sum of the differences between the mean and each score.

It is called the normal curve. Not all bell-shaped curves are normal, but the normal curve is important because many statistical techniques are based on the assumption that the graph of a large set of scores or data tends to approximate the normal curve.

The question of how this normal curve came to be is often asked. It was developed empirically. Various people made observations of physical characteristics such as the heights of mountains in a typical range or the measure of various bodily traits (height, weight, clothing sizes) or the values a group of people would get when each measured the same object. Finally, after many such observations were made, the normal curve came to be accepted as a picture of reality.

This is convenient because it allows the statistician to obtain characteristics of the population without having to poll or query or measure the whole population. Further, an individual score can be compared to the population to determine a ranking. The following chapters on dispersion and scores of relative standing will show specific uses of the properties of the normal curve.

REFERENCES

Noether, G. 1971. *Introduction to statistics: a fresh approach.* Boston: Houghton-Mifflin.

Salvia, J., and Ysseldyke, J. E. 1981. *Assessment in special and remedial education,* 2nd ed. Boston: Houghton-Mifflin.

Schmidt, M. 1975. *Understanding and using statistics: basic concepts.* Lexington, Massachusetts: D. C. Heath.

Walker, H. M. 1929. *Studies in the history of statistical method.* Baltimore: Williams and Wilkins.

CHAPTER 6

DISPERSION

Dispersion is also called the spread of scores or variability. It may be thought of as an indication of how much a set of scores spreads out above and below the measure of central tendency. As seen in Chapter 3, measures of central tendency are important as summary indicators of trends in sets of scores. There are other indicators of trends which are important descriptors. They are the range, quartile deviation, and standard deviation.

Range

The range is the difference between the highest score and lowest score in a set of scores. Although crude, it is simple to understand and obtain, and it provides a quick estimate of variability. When combined with the measures of central tendency, the range can provide some indication of the composition of a distribution. In the following sets of scores:

1. 7, 9, 11, 14, 15, 17, 50, 50, 50, 53, 55, 91, 92, 94
2. 43, 44, 45, 45, 47, 48, 50, 50, 50, 51, 52, 55, 56, 56, 56, 59
3. 12, 14, 41, 41, 42, 48, 50, 50, 50, 63, 65, 65, 66, 68, 68, 72

the means are equal to 50, the medians are equal to 50, and the modes are equal to 50. Each set of scores presents a different picture, however.

In the first set of scores, the range is 94 minus 7, or 87, and indicates a wide variety of competence in the area chosen for testing. The second set of scores has a range of 59 minus 43, or 16, and shows the group to be rather homogeneous with regard to the trait measured. A quick glance at the third set may lead one to make a conclusion similar to that reached about the first set. The range is 72 minus 12, or 60, but the conclusion is that the low scores of 12 and 14 somehow distort the picture. The quartile deviation would probably be a better descriptor in this case.

Quartile Deviation

The quartile deviation (Q) is also called the semi-interquartile range and is used with the median. Q describes dispersion differently than the range. To exclude deviancy at both ends of the distribution, the highest 25 percent of the scores and the lowest 25 percent of the scores are excluded. The range of the remaining 50 percent of the scores is found and this re-stricted range is divided by two to obtain a number in distance relationship with the median. To find Q in the following set of 16 scores, 12, 14, 41, 41, 42, 48, 50, 50, 50, 63, 65, 65 66, 68, 68, 72, first calculate that 25 percent of 16 is 4. Exclude 25 percent at the high score end and 25 percent at the low score end, leaving the set 42, 48, 50, 50, 50, 63, 65, 65. The range of this set is 65 minus 42, or 23. One-half of 23 is 23/2, or 11.5. Q in this ex-ample is equal to 11.5 and indicates that a large number of scores tends to cluster around the median plus or minus the quartile deviation. This relation-ship is expressed as

Mdn ± *Q* or 50 ± 11.5 or 38.5 to 61.5.

If the distribution is not normal because of a concentration of scores at some distance from the median or a single score at an extreme distance from the median, Q is the preferable descriptor. Examples of distributions which may be described by Q are:

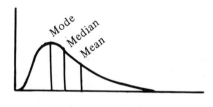

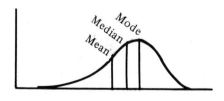

There is one other case in which Q is useful. If the scores are reported as percentiles, Q and the median are preferable to the mean and standard deviation as descriptors.

Standard Deviation

The normal curve was identified as a picture of typical distribution. This does not mean that every point contained by the curve is average or typical or indicative of normality. Within any bell-shaped curve are scores which deviate from the mean to a degree that they may be considered not typical of the group as a whole. The problem becomes one of setting limits so that the range of normality becomes defined numerically. Stated another way, one would ask what the cut-off points were. One way to set the cut-off points is through an arbitrary decision. If it were assumed that 50 percent or 66.6 percent or 75 percent or 91 percent of the population was normal, then one would merely find the points which contained the middle half, or two-thirds, or three-fourths, or whatever, of the population, and those points would be established as the cut-off points. Any score outside the range from low cut-off point to high cut-off point would be considered as an indication of abnormal behavior and dealt with in an appropriate manner. The obvious problem with this is deciding what percentage of the population is normal or typical. Is there a way to avoid making these kinds of arbitrary decisions and avoiding the inevitable debate of qualifications of the decision maker?

Fortunately, an examination of the normal curve is helpful. Researchers have carefully graphed normal curves and drawn tangents to the curve at various points. Theoretically, a tangent is a straight line which intersects a curved line at only one point. After many tangents were drawn, the slopes of the various tangent lines were calculated and compared.

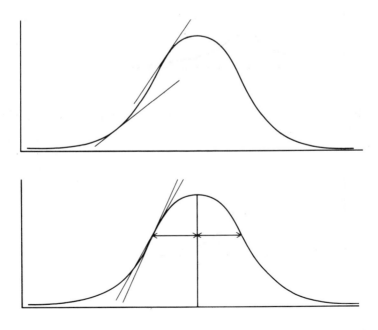

The slope is the rate at which a line ascends or descends. It was found that there were two points where the slopes of the tangents changed from being gradual to being steep. The points were at an equal distance from the mean and lay on either side of the mean. It was logical to assume that the part of the curve between these two points included typical or normal behavior. This method of defining normal behavior is an empirical method, one which relies on observation of phenomena.

There is another way to define normality in which it is not necessary to construct tangent lines and determine points by inspection. This second way is to calculate the standard deviation and establish points on the curve not dependent on tedious drawing or subject to error caused by graphing. It has been found that the normal curve depends on two numbers. One is the mean. If one were to fold the curve in half along the mean, the left half would fit exactly on the right half. The shape of each normal curve may be different, however, as in the following examples.

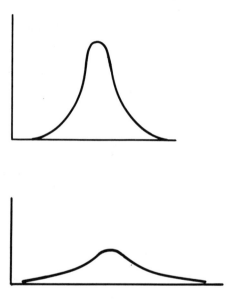

Even if the means and areas under the curves are equal, different shapes may result, as in this example:

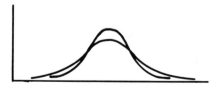

These different shapes result from variations in the spread of each curve. The measure of that spread is standard deviation (SD). Standard deviation indicates variation within a set of scores. It is the average of the degree to which a set of scores deviates from the mean. A smaller SD describes a curve that is taller and less spread-out than one with a larger SD.

Conceptually, SD is easy to understand. One merely needs to take each score, subtract it from the mean, and then find the average of these differences. Unfortunately, the system of mathematics in use will not allow this. Because the curve is symmetric about the mean, for every score below the mean there is a corresponding score above the mean. When one score is subtracted from the mean, the difference will be negative. When its corresponding score is subtracted from the mean, the difference will be positive. Because the curve is symmetric about the mean, the absolute value of the differences will be equal. But because one score is negative and one positive, the sum will always be zero. For every normal curve, the sum of the differences from the mean will be zero. Zero cannot be divided by the number of scores to find the average deviation, and therefore this method is useless because each normal curve, no matter what the shape, always has an average deviation of zero and cannot be differentiated from any other normal curve. An example of this is shown below:

$n = 25$

$\overline{X} = 100$

X	$X - \overline{X}$	$(X - \overline{X})^2$	X^2
65	−35	1225	4,225
70	−30	900	4,900
84	−16	256	7,056
85	−15	225	7,225
95	− 5	25	9,025
95	− 5	25	9,025
96	− 4	16	9,216
96	− 4	16	9,216
98	− 2	4	9,604
98	− 2	4	9,604
98	− 2	4	9,604
100	0	0	10,000
100	0	0	10,000
100	0	0	10,000
102	2	4	10,404
102	2	4	10,404
102	2	4	10,404
104	4	16	10,816
104	4	16	10,816
105	5	25	11,025
105	5	25	11,025
115	15	225	13,225
116	16	256	13,456
130	30	900	16,900
135	35	1225	18,225
2500	0	5400	255,400

$(\Sigma X)^2 = 6,250,000$

Average deviation $= \dfrac{\Sigma (X - \bar{X})}{n} = \dfrac{0}{25} = 0$

The problem is that the positive numbers cancel the negative numbers. After some thought, it was decided that the distances from the mean should be squared (each number difference is multiplied by itself). Because the square of any number is positive, the problem of the negative numbers cancelling the positive ones would be eliminated. The idea is to square the differences, perform the calculations (averages), and then find the square root of the average. In the preceding description, the calculations would be as follows:

Average deviation $= \sqrt{\dfrac{\Sigma (X - \bar{X})^2}{n}} = \dfrac{5400}{25} = 14.6969$

There is still a problem. Calculations are not usually based on the population because it is costly and time-consuming to collect data from each member of the population. Data are collected from each member of a sample which represents the population and these data are used to determine what the population looks like. Any time one tries to take a sample and describe a population, there is always the fear that the sample is not really representative of the population. If this is not the case, erroneous conclusions may be drawn. To minimize this error as much as possible, correction factors are included in the calculations. With the standard deviation formula, it is assumed that the standard deviation of the sample and the mean of the sample are fairly close to the population standard deviation and mean; the formula takes on the following form:

$SD = \sqrt{\dfrac{\Sigma (X - \bar{X})^2}{n - 1}}$

This formula may be tedious to use and to lessen the time it takes to calculate the standard deviation, another formula was derived. It is as follows:

$SD = \sqrt{\dfrac{n\Sigma X^2 - (\Sigma X)^2}{n(n - 1)}}$

Examples of the use of each are as follows:

$$SD = \sqrt{\frac{\Sigma(X - \overline{X})^2}{n-1}}$$

$$= \sqrt{\frac{5400}{25-1}}$$

$$= \sqrt{\frac{5400}{24}}$$

$$= \sqrt{225}$$

$$= 15$$

$$SD = \sqrt{\frac{n\Sigma X^2 - (\Sigma X)^2}{n(n-1)}}$$

$$= \sqrt{\frac{25(255,400) - 6,250,000}{25(25-1)}}$$

$$= \sqrt{\frac{6,385,000 - 6,250,000}{25(24)}}$$

$$= \sqrt{\frac{135,000}{600}} = \sqrt{225}$$

$$= 15$$

Normal behavior has been defined as the part of the normal curve between the point determined by the left-side SD (-1 SD) and that determined by the right-side SD ($+1$ SD). Normal behavior has also been defined as the part of the curve between the points where the slopes of the tangent lines change from being gradual to being steep. Fortunately, the points coincide, precluding the debate over which definition of normality is more correct.

Approximately 68 percent of the population falls in the -1 to $+1$ SD area. Often, people talk about the points beyond ± 1 SD. The most currently accepted definition for mental retardation states in part that the IQ score of a mentally retarded child must lie at 2 SD or farther below the mean. In reality, there are no points on the normal curve other than ± 1 SD where the slope of the tangent changes abruptly. There are no deviations other than ± 1 SD which can be derived mathematically. Any other numbers than ± 1 SD have been arrived at in an arbitrary fashion and as such are numbers of convenience. The only empirical or mathematical justification for these numbers has to do with standardization. If the distribution is normal, units of standard deviation always encompass the same percentage of the population or sample, no matter what the population or sample size or shape of the normal curve. For example, at -1 SD, 16 percent of the population or sample lies to the left and 84 percent lies to the right. At -2 SD, 2 percent of the population or sample lies to the left and 98 percent lies to the right. These figures have been confirmed both empirically and mathematically.

Empirically, the area under the curve between any two points expressed as a percentage of the area of the total curve corresponds to the percentage of the population earning scores between the two points. As an example, the area between ± 1 SD is about 68 percent of the total area under the normal curve; one knows, therefore, that about 68 percent of the scores fall between -1 SD and $+1$ SD.

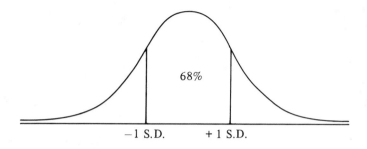

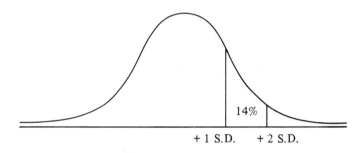

The area under the curve between +1 SD and +2 SD is 14 percent of the total, and one knows that 14 percent of the scores lie between the scores corresponding to +1 SD and +2 SD. Mathematically, formulas and tables have been constructed to confirm these relationships. They are beyond the scope of this text.

One other descriptor of curves is kurtosis. This is a system of classification based on the peakedness of curves. A mesokurtic curve is normal. A platykurtic curve is flattened. A leptokurtic curve has a high peak.

Problems

In the following problems, find the mean and standard deviation. Assume that each sample is representative of a normal population.

1. 1, 2, 2, 3, 3, 3, 4, 4, 5, 6
2. 1, 2, 3, 4, 5, 6, 7, 8
3. 4, 7, 8, 9, 9, 10, 10, 11, 12, 13
4. 1, 1, 1, 1, 1, 2, 2, 2, 3, 3, 3, 4, 5, 5, 5, 5, 5, 5, 5, 5, 5, 5, 6, 7, 7, 7, 7, 8, 8, 9

Answers

1. $n = 10$ $\Sigma X = 33$ $\overline{X} = 33/10 = 3.3$ $(\Sigma X)^2 = 1089$

$\Sigma X^2 = 1 + 4 + 4 + 9 + 9 + 9 + 16 + 16 + 25 + 36 = 129$

$$SD = \sqrt{\frac{n\,\Sigma X^2 - (\Sigma X)^2}{n(n-1)}} = \sqrt{\frac{10(129) - 1089}{10(9)}} = \sqrt{\frac{1290 - 1089}{90}}$$

$$= \sqrt{\frac{201}{90}} = \sqrt{2.23} = 1.49443$$

2. $n = 8$ $\Sigma X = 36$ $\overline{X} = 36/8 = 4.5$ $(\Sigma X)^2 = 1296$

$\Sigma X^2 = 1 + 4 + 9 + 16 + 25 + 36 + 49 + 64 = 204$

$$SD = \sqrt{\frac{n\Sigma X^2 - (\Sigma X)^2}{n(n-1)}} = \sqrt{\frac{8(204) - 1296}{8(7)}} = \sqrt{\frac{1632 - 1296}{56}}$$

$$= \sqrt{\frac{336}{56}} = \sqrt{6} = 2.44949$$

3. $n = 10$ $\Sigma X = 93$ $\overline{X} = 93/10 = 9.3$ $(\Sigma X)^2 = 8649$

$\Sigma X^2 = 16 + 49 + 64 + 81 + 81 + 100 + 100 + 121 + 144 + 169 = 925$

$$SD = \sqrt{\frac{n\Sigma X^2 - (\Sigma X)^2}{n(n-1)}} = \sqrt{\frac{10(925) - 8649}{10(9)}} = \sqrt{\frac{9250 - 8649}{90}}$$

$$= \sqrt{\frac{601}{90}} = \sqrt{6.67778} = 2.58414$$

4. $n = 30$ $\Sigma X = 133$ $\overline{X} = 133/30 = 4.4\overline{3}$ $(\Sigma X)^2 = 17{,}689$

$\Sigma X^2 = 1 + 1 + 1 + 1 + 1 + 1 + 4 + 4 + 4 + 9 + 9 + 9 + 16 + 25 + 25 + 25 + 25 + 25 + 25 + 25 + 25 + 25 + 25 + 49 + 49 + 49 + 49 + 64 + 64 + 81 = 751$

$$SD = \sqrt{\frac{n\Sigma X^2 - (\Sigma X)^2}{n(n-1)}} = \sqrt{\frac{30(751) - 17{,}689}{30(29)}} = \sqrt{\frac{22{,}530 + 17{,}689}{870}}$$

$$= \sqrt{\frac{4841}{870}} = \sqrt{5.56437} = 2.35889$$

REFERENCES

Anderson, T. R., and Zelditch, M. 1968. *A basic course in statistics,* 2nd ed. New York: Holt, Rinehart, and Winston.

Blank, S. S. 1968. *Descriptive statistics.* New York: Appleton Century Crofts.

CHAPTER 7

SCORES OF RELATIVE STANDING

All of these scores can be related to the two determinants of a normal curve—the mean and standard deviation. Each has been developed for a purpose which will be explained as each score is discussed. Standard deviation is used with the mean to describe the spread of scores in a group and to serve as the basis for computing standard scores.

Standard scores. Standard scores may be defined as those expressed in terms of their linear distance from the mean. Standard deviation is used as the unit of measure. This permits the conversion of raw scores to a common scale which has equal units and which can readily be interpreted in terms of the normal curve. By utilizing standard scores, a child's scores on various tests can be compared with each other. Each set of scores always has the same mean and the same standard deviation. Examples of standard scores are (1) z-score, (2) T-score, (3) deviation IQ, and (4) stanine.

Z-score

The z-score concept was developed as a way to convert any raw score to standard deviation units. Units of standard deviation are expressed as whole number distances from the mean, such as +1 SD or −2 SD. The standard deviation concept is easily understood, but whole numbers are not precise enough. It would be advantageous to be able to express scores as decimal equivalents, and the z-score does that. If a child earns a raw score of 84 on Test A and 116 on Test B, it is difficult to interpret the meaning of those scores. If the same scores were expressed as z-scores, the interpretation would be much easier. For purposes of discussion, assume that a raw score of 84 on Test A was equal to a z-score of +0.24 and that a raw score of 116 on Test B was equal to a z-score of −0.17. The educator would then know that this child scored slightly above the mean on Test A and slightly below the mean on Test B. Both scores are within the normal range. Remember that "normal" is defined mathematically as the range from −1 SD to +1 SD, or, expressed as z-scores, from −1.00 to +1.00. Another child might earn z-scores of −1.52 and −1.85. If these were intelligence tests, the child would not be eligible for placement in classes for the mentally retarded based on these scores. The recommended cut-off point is −2.00.

Besides being easy to understand as decimal equivalents of standard deviation, the z-score is easy to calculate. It is equal to the raw score minus the mean score divided by the standard deviation, or

$$z = \frac{X - \overline{X}}{SD}$$

The z-score always has a mean of zero and a standard deviation of one. An example is offered to illustrate the computation.

$\overline{X} = 47$ $X = 53$ $SD = 4$ Find z

$$z = \frac{X - \overline{X}}{SD} = \frac{53 - 47}{4} = 6/4 = +1.5$$

The score is significantly above average because it is above the average range of 43 to 51.

To gain facility with z-scores, the reader is encouraged to complete the following exercises:

					Answers
1.	$\overline{X} = 100$	$X = 120$	$SD = 15$	Find z	1.33
2.	$\overline{X} = 27$	$X = 24$	$SD = 3$	Find z	−1.00
3.	$\overline{X} = 50$	$X = 62$	$SD = 10$	Find z	1.20
4.	$\overline{X} = 76.3$	$X = 71$	$SD = 2.3$	Find z	−2.30

5. John scores 75 on a test with a mean of 60 and SD of 18. Joe scores 27 on a test with a mean of 24 and SD of 2. If both tests measure the same thing, which student did better? Answer: Joe did better because his z-score is higher.

John

$X = 75$ $\overline{X} = 60$ $SD = 18$

$$z = \frac{X - \overline{X}}{SD} = \frac{75 - 60}{18} = .833$$

Joe

$X = 27$ $\overline{X} = 24$ $SD = 2$

$$z = \frac{X - \overline{X}}{SD} = \frac{27 - 24}{2} = 1.5$$

T-score

The T-score is very similar to the z-score. One of the disadvantages of using z-scores to many people is the use of negative numbers. Another disadvantage is the use of decimals. Because many people feel more comfortable working with whole positive numbers, the T-score was developed. It is a standard score with a mean of 50 and a standard deviation of 10. A T-score is found by multiplying the z-score by 10, rounding to the nearest whole number, and adding 50 to the result. An example of the calculation follows:

Convert the z-score -3.71 to a T-score.
$T = 10$ (z-score) $+ 50 = -37.1 + 50 = -37 + 50 = 13$.

Actually, any z-score may be converted to a score with any mean and standard deviation if the scores are normally distributed. The formula for this is known as the sigma-score formula and is

$$SS = X_{ss} + (SD_{ss}) (z\text{-score}) \qquad SS = X_{ss} + (SD_{ss}) (z\text{-score})$$

where SS is the sigma score,
X_{ss} is the mean of the new distribution,
SD_{ss} is the standard deviation of the new distribution, and the z-score is the score being converted.

If $X_{ss} = 50$ and $SD_{ss} = 10$, SS is expressed as a T-score. To illustrate, the sigma-score formula will be used to convert a z-score of $+0.79$ to a T-score.

$$
\begin{aligned}
SS &= \overline{X}_{ss} + (SD_{ss}) (z) \\
&= 50 + 10 (.79) \\
&= 50 + 7.9 = 57.9 \\
&= 58
\end{aligned}
$$

If the mean were to be 100 and the standard deviation 15, the calculations would be as follows for computing a z-score of -0.43.

$$
\begin{aligned}
SS &= \overline{X}_{ss} + (SD_{ss}) (z) \\
&= 100 + 15 (-.43) \\
&= 100 + (-6.45) \\
&= 100 - 6.45 \\
&= 93.55 = 94
\end{aligned}
$$

Here the standard score would not be a T-score. If a T-score was desired for the z-score of -0.43, it would be calculated as follows:

$$
\begin{aligned}
SS &= \overline{X}_{ss} + (SD_{ss}) (z) & &= 50 - 4.3 \\
&= 50 + 10 (-.43) & &= 45.7 = 46
\end{aligned}
$$

The following exercises are offered for practice.

1. Find the T-score when the z-score is -1.2.
2. Find the standard score with mean of 500 and standard deviation of 100 when the z-score is 0.47.

3. A *T*-score is given as 36. Find the *z*-score.
4. A standard score of 575 is given with the mean as 500 and the standard deviation as 100. What is the *z*-score?

Answers

1. $SS = \overline{X}_{ss} + (SD_{ss})(z)$

   $= 50 + 10(-1.2)$
   $= 50 - 12$
   $= 38$

2. $SS = \overline{X}_{ss} + (SD_{ss})(z)$

   $= 500 + 100(-.47)$
   $= 500 + 47$
   $= 547$

3. $SS = \overline{X}_{ss} + (SD_{ss})(z)$

   $36 = 50 + 10(z)$
   $10z = -14$
   $z = -1.4$

4. $SS = \overline{X}_{ss} + (SD_{ss})(z)$

   $575 = 500 + 100(z)$
   $100(z) = 75$
   $z = .75$

Deviation IQ

Deviation IQ is a relatively new concept. It supercedes the ratio IQ with which most people are familiar, but which is now considered obsolete. The deviation IQ and ratio IQ are derived from different assumptions. Both will be discussed.

The ratio IQ is based on an age equivalent schema. First, a child's mental age (MA) is found through testing. These tests are constructed in the following manner: At each age, a sample of children is collected. There may be, say, 200 children who are five years old, 200 who are six, 200 who are seven, and so on. Each group is given the same test, and the raw scores for each group age are calculated. After that, the mean score for each age is graphed, and a line of best fit is used to connect the points. Simplified, it looks like this:

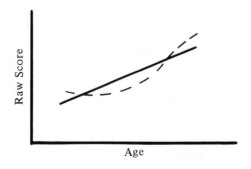

These average scores represent the raw score equivalents for each age level. For instance, assume the five-year-olds had a mean score of 400, the six-year-olds a mean score of 450, the seven-year-olds a mean score of 521, and so on. The mean score is the raw score equivalent of the mental age for each group. Using the preceding example, if a six-year-old earned a raw score of 450, his mental age would be six years. If another six-year-old earned a score of 520, the examiner would have to search to find the age level at which a score of 520 was average. In this case, this occurs at age seven; therefore, this six-year-old has a mental age of seven. Graphically, it looks like this:

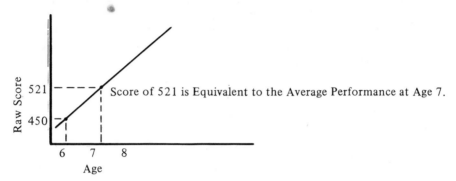

The IQ is calculated from the mental age through use of the following formula:

$$IQ = \frac{MA}{CA} \times 100,$$

where MA is the mental age in months and CA is the chronological age of the child in months. For the two examples cited above, the calculations are as follows:

CA = 6 years = 72 months

Raw score = 450 and equals
    an MA of 6 years or 72 months

IQ = MA/CA × 100
   = 72/72 × 100 = 100

CA = 6 years = 72 months

Raw score = 520 and equals
    an MA of 7 years or 84 months

IQ =MA/CA × 100
   = 84/72 × 100 = 117

The ratio IQ was developed with the assumption that intellectual growth is linear (occurs at a steady rate). This may not be true. There is evidence that indicates that children grow mentally in spurts and plateaus. If that is the case, the standard deviation at each age range is not equal. This could cause fluctuations in IQ scores of a child from year to year which are not really present.

Several other problems arise in using this method to determine IQ. The methods of calculating the ratio IQ are suspect because, with the same data, it is possible to arrive at different mental ages. One method of calculating MA, described in following paragraphs, is to first break the sample into age levels and find the mean score at each age. Another way that can be used to calculate MA is to take a score and find the average age of the group of children who earn that score. This process is repeated for each score range and will probably yield different MAs than the other method.

Another problem has to do with children who earn extreme scores— either very high or very low. With ratio IQ, these children are assigned mental ages which are farther from the mean than their "true" MAs.

There is also a misconception regarding the interpretation of the meaning of IQ. In the past, the ratio IQ has mistakenly been thought of as the level of growth of a particular individual. Actually, a ratio IQ yields the rate of mental development. For example, an IQ of 120 at age 10 indicates a rate of growth of 1.2 years for each chronological year. This is seen through use of the ratio IQ formula,

$$IQ = MA/CA \times 100.$$

Substituting, the values are

$$120 = MA/120 \times 100.$$

By transposition,

$$MA = 120 \times 120/100 = 144 = 12 \text{ years.}$$

Then, years of mental growth per chronological age equals MA/CA or 144/120 or 1.2. In intellectual development, people tend to level off in growth at about age 16 or so and reach a plateau of mental power. The problem is obvious. If a bright 14-year-old earns a high raw score, there will be no age group at which her score is average; it is not possible to determine an accurate mental age for this youngster. Another possible interpretation is that, because there is a leveling off in growth, the IQ should be around zero for adults. It appears that the ratio IQ means different things at different ages. At any rate, much confusion results when the ratio concept is used.

One more problem is evident in using the ratio IQ concept. Because, say, a five-year-old and a twelve-year-old could earn the same mental age, the logical assumption is that both function alike. This conclusion could not be farther from the truth. Five-year-olds and twelve-year-olds do not act alike and are not at the same point of physical and psychological development. Age is a factor which cannot be minimized.

To deal with these problems, the deviation IQ was developed. As in finding the ratio IQ, raw scores at each chronological age are collected. The difference is that there is no comparison across age levels. The performance of each five-year-old is compared against only other five-year-olds; each score of those at age six is compared to the scores earned by the other six-year-olds, and so on. At each age level, a normal curve emerges and the mean and standard deviation are calculated. These raw score means and standard deviations are converted to standard scores, ususally with a mean of 100 and standard deviation of 15 or 16. Thus, any raw score may be converted to a standard score and this standard score is the IQ. An example problem is given here. Problem: Find the IQ when the raw score is 420, the raw score mean is 450, and the raw score standard deviation is 70. Answer: The problem may be solved through use of the z-score formula and the sigma-score formula. First find the z-score:

$$z = (X - \overline{X})/SD = (420 - 450)/70 = -.43.$$

Then find the standard score with mean of 100 and SD of 15:

$$SS = \overline{X}_{ss} + (SD_{ss})(z) = 100 + 15(-.43) = 100 + (-6.45) = 93.55 = 94.$$

In this example the IQ score is 94.

One great advantage of this method is that fluctuations in IQ are greatly reduced. In the course of normal development, children are assumed to progress in a somewhat erratic fashion, but are thought to maintain the same position relative to others of the same age.

Because scores are derived from within age ranges, there is only one way to calculate IQ. This eliminates a great deal of ambiguity.

With any normal distribution, there can be problems with extreme scores. This is partly because there are very few extreme scores and it is difficult to draw meaningful conclusions from a small sample. One of the most frustrating tasks in statistical life is to describe the retardate who scores at IQ 28 or the genius who scores at IQ 151. Perhaps the only solution is to construct tests based on extremely high or low scores.

The deviation IQ puts a group of people in relation to each other; it is thereby a measure of some factors in intellectual power and not rate of mental growth. Again, ambiguity is reduced because IQ now has the same meaning at any age.

Finally, the deviation IQ takes into account the fact that it is difficult to compare children meaningfully across ages. It is more fair to reduce the variables of physiological, emotional, and psychological differences based on age by minimizing age as a variable.

Stanine

The stanine is somewhat different from other standard scores. Stanine is an acronym for standard scores of nine units or "standard nines." Normal distribution is broken down into nine parts as follows:

Stanine	Approximate z-score or S.D. units			Percent of cases	Designation
1	$-\infty$	to	-1.75	4.01	very low
2	-1.75	to	-1.25	6.55	very low
3	-1.25	to	$-.75$	12.10	low
4	$-.75$	to	$-.25$	17.47	low average
5	$-.25$	to	$+.25$	19.74	average
6	$+.25$	to	$+.75$	17.47	high average
7	$+.75$	to	$+1.25$	12.10	high
8	$+1.25$	to	$+1.75$	6.55	very high
9	$+1.75$	to	$+\infty$	4.01	very high

This scale was developed at a time when it was difficult to store large amounts of data for computer use. The only format available was the standard IBM card with an 80-column capacity. Each test score took up at least two columns of space. If this could be cut down to one column, at least twice as many test scores could be reported in the same space. Through use of stanines, the military was able to index data to a single-digit number and gain in efficiency in its Air Force Aviation Psychology Program in World War II.

Stanines are still in use today. Many people have criticized this scale because it is confusing. Although based on a normal distribution, there is no empirical or mathematical justification for the divisions. The designation "average" has a different meaning when stanines are used as opposed to standard deviation units. The use of stanines has been criticized because the categories give only a rough approximation of standing, especially in the case of measures having high reliability. This deficiency is usually referred to as a loss of information. The advantages of using stanines are generally thought to be outweighed by the disadvantages.

The Quantile Family

Included here are percentiles or centiles, deciles, and quartiles. Precision is the major difference among the scores.

Percentiles. Percentiles have been defined in three different ways.

1. The percentage of scores in a set which fall below a given score.
2. The percentage of scores in a set which fall at or below a given score.
3. The percentage of scores in a set which fall below the midpoint of a given score interval. This is becoming the most accepted definition.

When a large number of scores is reported (a large distribution), the differences in percentile scores across the three definitions tend to be minimized. With relatively small samples, the percentile score could be quite variable, depending on which definition was used. Consider the following example.

Score	Percentile Score by Definition		
	Below	*At or Below*	*Below Midpoint*
10	80	100	90
7	60	80	70
6	40	60	50
4	20	40	30
2	0	20	10

When the definitions are literally interpreted, percentiles are calculated through use of the following formulae:

Where

Below $\qquad PR = B/n \times 100$ $\qquad PR$ = percentile score or rank

$\qquad\qquad\qquad\qquad\qquad\qquad\qquad\qquad X$ = the raw score

At or Below $\quad PR = (B+E)/n \times 100$ $\qquad B$ = the number of scores below X

$\qquad\qquad\qquad\qquad\qquad\qquad\qquad\qquad E$ = the number of scores equal to X

Below Midpoint $PR = (B + \tfrac{1}{2}E)/n \times 100$ $\qquad n$ = the total number of scores

In the event of decimals, round to the nearest whole number.

Percentiles have several distinct advantages. They are computed fairly easily and can be converted to standard scores as illustrated by the following table:

SD	−3	−2	−1	0	+1	+2	+3
Percentile	.1	2	16	50	84	98	99.9

They may also be easily understood and for purposes of explanation may be reported as the percentage of scores below a given score. At a percentile of 42, it can be stated that 42 percent of the people scored below and 58 percent scored above the referent.

With percentiles, a pupil's performance is reported in relation to others of the group of which he is a member. Performance can also be predicted by comparing a score to other scores earned by the group to which the referent seeks membership. For example, the normal range in percentile scores extends from the 16th percentile to the 84th percentile. A regular curriculum should be able to accommodate the 68 percent of the population scoring within this range. Therefore, if a special education student scores in the 25th percentile on a test or subtest of, say, reading comprehension, that student should be able to function in the regular class in that area.

One must be very careful, when using percentiles, to refer to the norm group on which the percentiles were computed. This is because percentile scores are scores of relative standing and performance reported as a score in one group may be interpreted quite differently when the group is composed of individuals with different traits. For example, in an achievement test, a student in third grade who earns a raw score of 14 may be placed at the 40th percentile. That same raw score of 14 earned by a fifth-grader may be at only the 23rd percentile. The difference is that fifth-graders are expected to achieve at a higher level. This is why a percentile can never be reported alone, but must always be reported with a description of the group from which the scores were derived.

Some confusion has arisen with percentile scores because they represent an unequal interval. Because scores are assumed to be normally distributed, there is a large cluster about the mean and a regular drop-off in frequency away from the mean. Because percentiles are scores of relative standing and because there is a large cluster of scores about the mean, percentile differences near the mean represent much smaller raw score interval differences than percentile differences away from the mean. This point is illustrated in the following hypothetical test score distribution:

Raw Score	58	71	97	107	111	115	117	118	123	128	137	153	169
Percentile	20	25	30	35	40	45	50	55	60	65	70	75	80

As a result of this characteristic of percentiles, small differences in percentile scores near the middle of the distribution are not as important as those same differences at the extremes. Generally, a student scoring at the 45th percentile needs only to increase his raw score total by a few points to achieve the 50th or 55th percentile, while a raw score equal to the 75th percentile must be raised substantially to achieve the 80th percentile. If one keeps in mind that percentiles are scores of relative standing, this limitation should not cause difficulty. Another limitation of percentiles is that they are not additive and cannot be averaged because the intervals between percentile scores are not equal. If calculations involving addition, subtraction, division, or multiplication are necessary, the percentiles should be converted to standard scores and the calculations performed on these equal interval scores.

Quartiles and deciles. The quantile family also includes quartiles and deciles. Quartiles are defined as the points which divide a distribution into four equal parts and are the 25th percentile (Q_1), the 50th percentile or median (*Mdn*), and the 75th percentile (Q_3). Deciles divide a distribution into ten equal parts and are the 10th, 20th, 30th, 40th, 50th, 60th, 70th, 80th, and 90th percentiles. Both quartiles and deciles may be found by counting or, especially in the case where scores are reported in intervals as in a frequency distribution, by formula. Several examples follow:

In the following distribution, find Q_1, Q_3, and P_{70} or D_7

5, 6, 7, 8, 9, 13, 17, 21, 31, 33, 39, 41, 44, 47, 48, 52, 54, 55, 58, 59

n = total number of scores = 20

Mdn = ½ of 20 = the point at which 10 scores lie above and 10 scores lie below. It is the point between score number 10 and score number 11 or $(33 + 39)/2 = 36$

Q_1 is the point where 25 percent or 5 of the scores lie below and 75 percent or 15 lie above. It lies between the fifth and sixth scores and is found in a similar fashion as the median or $(9 + 13)/2 = 11$.

Q_3 is the point where 75 percent or 15 of the scores lie below and 25 percent of the scores lie above and is $(48 + 52)/2$ or 50.

P_{70} or D_7 is the point where 70 percent of the scores lie below and 30 percent lie above. Here $P_{70} = (47 + 48)/2 = 47.5$.

In the following distribution, find Mdn, Q_1, Q_3, and P_{60}

Class Interval	98–100	95–97	92–94	89–91	86–88	83–85	80–82	77–79
Frequency	1	2	0	2	1	7	9	8

Class Interval	74–76	71–73	68–70	65–67
Frequency	4	3	2	1

In the case of a frequency distribution, the points must be estimated through the use of formulae,

$$Mdn = L_{Mdn} + \frac{n/2 - S}{f_{Mdn}} \times i$$

Where n = the total number of scores
$$= 1 + 2 + 0 + 2 + 1 + 7 + 9 + 8 + 4 + 3 + 2 + 1 = 40$$

L_{Mdn} is equal to the lowest possible limit for the median. Here the median is between the twentieth and twenty-first score ($Mdn = 40/2 = 20$; twenty scores lie above and twenty below the Mdn) and lies somewhere in the interval 80–82. In that interval the lowest point is 80 and the limits of 80 are 80.5 and 79.5 (scores are assumed to be continuous) = 79.5. S is equal to the number of scores in the intervals below L, or $8 + 4 + 3 + 2 + 1 = 18$. f_{Mdn} is equal to the number of scores in the Mdn interval, or 9. i is equal to the size of the intervals, or 3.

Here the $Mdn = 79.5 + \dfrac{40/2 - 18}{9} \times 3 = 80.37$ Where L_{Q_1} is between the 10th and 11th score and f_{Q_1} is the number of scores in the Q_1 interval (8).

$$Q_1 = L_{Q_1} + \frac{n/4 - S}{f_{Q_1}} \times i$$

$$Q_1 = 76.5 + \frac{40/4 - 10}{8} \times 3$$

$$= 76.5 + 0 = 76.5$$

$$Q_3 = L_{Q_3} + \frac{3n/4 - S}{f_{Q_1}} \times i$$ Where L_{Q_3} is between the thirtieth and thirty-first score.

$$Q_3 = 82.5 + \frac{3(40) - 27}{7} \times 3$$

$$= 82.5 + 3/7(3)$$

$$= 82.5 + 1.2857 = 83.7857 = 83.8$$

$$P_{60} = L_{P_{60}} + \frac{6n/10 - S}{f_{L_{P_{60}}}} \times 3$$

Where $L_{P_{60}}$ is the point where 24 scores lie below and 16 scores lie above $(6/10 \times 40)$

$$= 79.5 = \frac{6(40)/10 - 18}{9} \times 3$$

$$= 79.5 + 6/9\,(3) = 79.5 + 2 = 81.5$$

In the following distribution, find Q_1, Mdn, and P_{30}: 41, 42, 42, 43, 44, 45, 46, 46, 46, 46, 46, 48, 51, 51, 51, 51, 53, 54, 54, 57, 58, 58, 59. To find the median, count until an equal number of scores are above and below a point. Here the 12th score is the median because 11 scores lie above and 11 scores lie below. The median is 48.

The median can also be found by formula and this has been done for purposes of illustration.

$$Mdn = L_{Mdn} + \frac{n/2 - S}{f_{L_{Mdn}}} \times i$$

Where the twelfth score lies in the interval 47.5 to 48.5.

$$= 47.5 + \frac{23/2 - 11}{1} \times 1$$

$$= 47.5 + .5/1 = 47.5 + .5 = 48.0$$

Q_1 is the point at which 25 percent of the scores lie below and 75 percent lie above. This is not possible to determine by instpection, so this point will be found through calculation. To find the score corresponding to Q_1, multiply 23 by 25 percent to obtain 5.75. Q_1 lies somewhere between the 5th and 6th scores. By interpolation, Q_1 is the point which is the 5th point plus .75 of the distance between the 5th and 6th points, or .75 (45 – 44), which is equal to .75. The point is 44 + .75, or 44.75.

P_{30} is also found by interpolation. It is the point which corresponds to 3/10 (23) and equals 6.9. P_{30} is the sixth score in the distribution plus 9/10 of the interval between the sixth and seventh scores. $P_{30} = 45 + 9/10\,(46 - 45) = 45.9$.

Problems

For the next five problems, use the distribution 1, 1, 2, 8, 9, 9, 9, 9, 11, 17, 18, 21, 30, 32, 32, 33, 33, 33, 34, 34, 34, 35, 36, 36, 38, 41, 47, 47, 48, 48, 49, 49, 50, 50, 50, 51, 57, 59, 60, 61, 65, 66, 66, 67, 68.

1. What are the percentile equivalents of the raw scores 9, 36, 51, 66, 68?
2. Find the *Mdn*.
3. Where is the third quartile?

4. What is P_{70}?
5. What is P_{35}?

For the next three problems, use the frequency distribution:

Scores	6–10	11–15	16–20	21–25	26–30	31–35	36–40	41–45
Frequency	1	2	4	7	5	3	2	1

6. Find the *Mdn.*
7. Find Q_3.
8. What is P_{90}?

Answers

1. $PR = (B + \frac{1}{2}E)/n \times 100$
   for raw score 9, $PR = (4 + \frac{1}{2}[4])/45 \times 100 = 600/45 = 13$
   for raw score 36, $PR = (22 + \frac{1}{2}[2])/45 \times 100 = 2300/45 = 51$
   for raw score 51, $PR = (35 + \frac{1}{2}[1])/45 \times 100 = 3550/45 = 79$
   for raw score 66, $PR = (41 + \frac{1}{2}[2])/45 \times 100 = 4200/45 = 93$
   for raw score 68, $PR = (44 + \frac{1}{2}[1])/45 \times 100 = 4450/45 = 99$

2. The *Mdn* is found by counting. It is the point where 22 scores lie above and 22 scores lie below. There, it is the 23rd score, or 36.

3. $Q_3 = \frac{3}{4} \times 45 = 33.75$. Q_3 is 75/100 of the distance between the 33rd and 34th scores. Here the 33rd score is 50 and the 34th score is 50 and therefore $Q_3 = 50$.

4. $P_{70} = 7/10 \times 45 = 31.5$. P_{70} is $\frac{1}{2}$ the distance between the 31st and 32nd score. Here the equation would be $49 + \frac{1}{2}(50 - 49) = 49.5$.

5. $P_{35} = 35/100 \times 45 = 15.75$. P_{35} is $\frac{3}{4}$ of the way between the 15th and 16th scores. Here the equation would be $32 + \frac{3}{4}(33 - 32) = 32.5$.

6. $Mdn = L_{Mdn} + (n/2 - S)/f \times i = 20.5 + (25/2 - 7)/7 \times 5 = 24.43$.

7. $Q_3 = L_{Q_3} + (3n/4 - S)/f \times i = 25.5 + (3[25]/4 - 14)/5 \times 5$
   $= 30.25$.

8. $P_{90} = L_{P_{90}} + (9n/10 - S)/f \times i = 35.5 + (9[25]/10 - 22)/2 \times 5$
   $= 36.75$.

REFERENCES

Blank, S. S. 1968. *Descriptive statistics.* New York: Appleton Century Crofts.

Ebel, R. L. 1972. *Essentials of educational measurement.* Englewood Cliffs, New Jersey: Prentice-Hall.

Gronlund, N. E. 1971. *Measurement and evaluation in teaching,* 2nd ed. New York: Macmillan.

Thorndike, R. L. (ed.). 1971. *Educational measurement,* 2nd ed. Washington, D. C.: American Council on Education.

Vodola, T. M. 1974. *Descriptive statistics made easy for the classroom teacher.* Bloomfield, New Jersey: C. F. Wood.

CHAPTER 8

RELIABILITY

Up to this point the discussion has centered around the behavior of, and the operations which could be performed on, one variable. The reader should be able to describe a group of test scores in several ways in relation to the normal curve. An assumption which is made is that the distribution of scores from a representative sample is a picture or model of the distribution of scores which would appear if the scores of each person in the population were collected. It is necessary to have some understanding of descriptive statistics involving one variable if an understanding of why a test is useful or not useful is to be gained.

It is only now that the problem of judging a test can be discussed. Three factors are associated with good tests. They are reliability, validity, and norming. Both reliability and validity involve making comparisons of test performance with another indicator of quality, such as another test or the same test. There are several types of reliability, but all involve the comparison of two continuous scores through the use of the Pearson product-moment correlation coefficient (r). This method of comparison depends upon techniques used in calculations with one variable, but goes a step beyond. In this chapter, correlation will be discussed as a concept before the types of reliability are discussed.

Correlation

Correlation is a measure of the degree of relationship of two variables or traits. As an example, consider the graphs of Trait 1 and Trait 2:

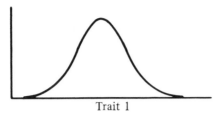

Trait 1

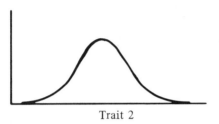

Trait 2

With these graphs, either trait may be described in terms of mean and standard deviation. Scores of relative standing may be computed and compared. With this information, the question of relationship cannot be answered.

A measure of "co-relation" is needed. If it happens that people exhibiting a high degree of Trait 1 also exhibit a high degree of Trait 2, a positive co-relation is evident. If those exhibiting a high degree of Trait 1 almost always exhibit a high degree of Trait 2 and those exhibiting a low degree of Trait 1 almost always exhibit a low degree of Trait 2, that is high positive co-relation. On the other hand, if high Trait 1 people tend to be low Trait 2 people, that is negative co-relation. If it is not possible to predict Trait 2 when Trait 1 is known, there is little or no relationship, and that situation is referred to as low or no co-relation.

Co-relation has been amended to correlation, but it may be easier to understand the concept if the reader mentally substitutes the term co-relation whenever the term correlation is encountered. An example involving tests will be given and then correlation will be discussed conceptually.

If two tests are given to a group and the people who earn high scores on one test also earn high scores on the second test and those who earn low scores on the first test also earn low scores on the second test, then the test scores are said to be positively correlated. In this relationship, the test scores (variables) both change in a regular manner with respect to each other. Another example of this regular change is negative correlation. The test scores would tend to be inversely related. If one earned a high score on the first test, it would be predictable that the score earned on the second test would be low.

Often, knowing one test score is of no help when it comes to predicting a score on a second test. In this situation, the scores have low correlation or no correlation.

There is a mathematical way of defining the degree of relationship between two variables. In fact, there are a number of ways to calculate correlation. These are determined by the type of data collected. All are based on finding abstract relationships, and all are arbitrary procedures which yield a single number which indicates the degree of relationship between two variables. As a result of the abstract nature of this statistic, it is not possible to describe it graphically. A picture just does not exist.

The most common measure of correlation in use is called the Pearson product-moment correlation coefficient and is symbolized by r. The development of this correlation coefficient will be traced through an example.

Suppose twenty people each took two tests—Test A and Test B. Their scores were as follows:

Name:	Lynn	Jim	John	Mary	Mark	Joe	Phyllis	Ann	Barb	Larry
Test A:	42	45	73	91	27	63	24	81	53	87
Test B:	46	51	84	84	32	55	19	85	51	79

Name:	Bill	Jane	Eric	Phil	Debbie	Paul	Alan	Ed	Pete	Helen
Test A:	10	23	36	64	51	38	27	14	45	37
Test B:	14	27	29	61	47	41	29	18	51	35

There are several ways to ask a question concerning the relationship of these scores. Does the score from Test A give an indication or prediction of the score on Test B? If a person earned a score of 38 on Test A, what would be a likely score for that person on Test B?

Researchers will often locate the points on a scatter plot to see if a pattern emerges. In this case, the pattern when one encircles the points is an oval tilted at roughly a 45-degree angle to either axis. By inspection, it is seen that low scores are associated with low scores and high scores with high scores in a more or less regular fashion. This is interesting, but not precise enough. If a line could be fitted through these points, it would allow one to predict a score on, say, Test B when a score on Test A was given.

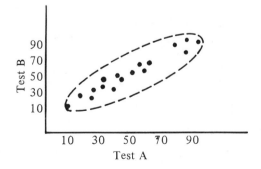

This is because a line takes the form of the equation $Y = bX + a$, where Y is the score on Test B, b is the slope of the line drawn through the points, a is a constant used to help locate the line on the graph, and X is the score on Test A. To predict what the score on Test B would be when a score on Test A was known, simply substitute the known values and solve for Y.

The question of how to fit a line through the points is crucial. The line of fit must be one which assures that the points calculated from the equation are as close as possible to the obtained (plotted) points. One way to obtain an equation is to draw a line and then calculate the values for a and b. This is difficult because different people will locate the line in different positions, and there is no guarantee that the drawn line is the most accurate line.

Probably the most accurate way to obtain this line of best fit is to use a method that insures that the average distance from the plotted points to their corresponding line points is the minimum distance possible. Here the same problem is encountered as in finding standard deviation in a normal distribution. Because there exists an equal amount of distances below the line (negative distances) as above (positive distances), the sum of the distances will always be zero. The same solution used to eliminate this problem with standard deviation can be used in this case also. The distances are squared and the calculations are made. This method is called the least-squares method and will be illustrated as follows:

Test Scores

$A(X)$	$B(Y)$	A^2	B^2	AB	$X-\bar{X}$	$Y-\bar{Y}$	$(X-\bar{X})^2$	$(Y-\bar{Y})^2$	$(X-\bar{X})(Y-\bar{Y})$
42	46	1764	2116	1932	- 4.55	- 0.9	20.7	0.81	0.4095
45	51	2025	2601	2295	- 1.55	4.1	2.4	16.81	- 6.355
73	84	5329	7056	6132	26.45	37.1	699.6	1376.41	981.295
91	84	8281	7056	7644	44.45	37.1	1975.8	1376.41	1649.1
27	32	729	1024	864	-19.55	-14.9	382.2	222.01	291.295
63	55	3969	3025	3465	16.45	8.1	270.6	65.61	133.245
24	19	576	361	456	-22.55	-27.9	508.5	778.41	629.145
81	85	6561	7225	6885	34.45	38.1	1186.8	1451.61	1312.55
53	51	2809	2601	2703	6.45	4.1	41.6	16.81	26.445
87	79	7569	6241	6873	40.45	32.1	1636.2	1030.41	1298.45
10	14	100	196	140	-36.55	-32.9	1335.9	1082.41	1202.5
23	27	529	729	621	-23.55	-19.9	554.6	396.01	468.645
36	29	1296	841	1044	-10.55	-17.9	111.3	320.41	188.845
64	61	4096	3721	3904	17.45	14.1	304.5	198.81	246.045
51	47	2601	2209	2397	4.45	- 0.1	19.8	0.01	- 0.445
38	41	1444	1681	1558	- 8.55	- 5.9	73.1	34.81	50.445
27	29	729	841	783	-19.55	-17.9	382.2	320.41	349.945
14	18	196	324	252	-32.55	-28.9	1059.5	835.21	940.695
45	51	2025	2601	2295	- 1.55	4.1	2.4	16.81	- 6.355
37	35	1369	1225	1296	- 9.55	-11.9	91.2	141.61	113.546
931	938	53,997	53,674	53,539	0.00	0.0	10,658.9	9681.80	9869.54

$$\begin{array}{cc} A\ (X) & B\ (Y) \\ \overline{X}\ =\ 46.55 & 46.9 \end{array}$$

$$SD\ =\ 23.0856 \quad 22.002$$

$$Y = bX + a \quad \text{where } b = \frac{\Sigma(X-\overline{X})(Y-\overline{Y})}{\Sigma(X-\overline{X})^2} \text{ and } a = \overline{Y} - b\overline{X}$$

$$b = \frac{9869.54}{10658.9} \qquad a = 46.9 - .92594\,(46.55)$$

$$= .92594 \qquad\qquad\quad = 46.9 - 43.1025$$

$$\text{or } .93 \qquad\qquad\quad = 3.7975$$

$$\text{or } 3.8$$

$$Y = .93X + 3.8$$

This line has been constructed to predict a Y score (Test B score) when an X score (Test A score) is known. In like manner, a second line can be constructed to predict an X score when a Y score is known.

$$X = bY + a \quad \text{where } b = \frac{\Sigma(X-\overline{X})(Y-\overline{Y})}{\Sigma(Y-\overline{Y})^2} \text{ and } a = \overline{X} - b\overline{Y}$$

$$b = \frac{9869.54}{9681.80} \qquad a = 46.55 - 1.01939\,(46.9)$$

$$= 1.01939 \qquad\qquad = 46.55 - 47.8094$$

$$= -1.2594$$

$$X = 1.02Y - 1.3$$

With this information, if a score of 38 were earned on Test A (X), the predicted score on Test B (Y) would be found by substituting known values into the equation

$$Y = bX + a$$
$$= .93\,(38) + 3.8 = 35.34 + 3.8$$
$$= 39.14 = 39$$

If a score of 38 was obtained on Test B (Y), the predicted score on Test A (X) would be found as follows:

$$X = bY + a$$
$$= 1.02\,(38) - 1.3$$
$$= 38.76 - 1.3$$
$$= 37.46 = 37$$

These lines are called regression lines or lines of best fit. They are measures of the functional relationship between the two variables. As such, they are expressions of average relationship. With this information it is still not possible to judge the magnitude of the relationship precisely. It is logical to assume that knowing the magnitude of dispersion about each line of best fit would help. This measure of dispersion is a standard deviation. When used with regression lines, it is called the standard error of estimate because it is a measure of the average distance of the true score from the scores predicted (estimated) from the line of best fit. For the example used earlier, the calculations for finding the standard error of estimate for each regression line would be as follows:

$$Y = .93X + 3.8 \qquad\qquad X = 1.02Y - 1.3$$

$$\mathrm{SD}_{Y \bullet X} = \sqrt{\frac{\Sigma(Y-\overline{Y})^2 - b[\Sigma(X-\overline{X})(Y-\overline{Y})]}{n-2}} \qquad \mathrm{SD}_{X \bullet Y} = \sqrt{\frac{\Sigma(X-\overline{X})^2 - b[\Sigma(X-\overline{X})(Y-\overline{Y})]}{n-2}}$$

$$= \sqrt{\frac{9681.8 - .92594\,(9869.54)}{18}} \qquad = \sqrt{\frac{10658.9 - 1.01939(9869.54)}{18}}$$

$$= \sqrt{\frac{9681.8 - 9138.6}{18}} \qquad\qquad = \sqrt{\frac{10658.9 - 10060.9}{18}}$$

$$\qquad\qquad\qquad\qquad = \sqrt{\frac{598}{18}} = \sqrt{33.2222}$$

$$= \sqrt{\frac{543.2}{18}} = \sqrt{30.1778} \qquad\qquad = 5.76387$$

$$= 5.49343$$

At this point, two regression lines and two standard errors of estimate have been calculated. Yet a measure of the magnitude of relationship between scores on Test A and Test B is still lacking. There is a way to obtain that measure, and it is described here.

The line of best fit is a predictor of Y when X is known or of X when Y is known. As the values of X and Y become more related, the lines of best fit yield calculated values which are closer to the actual values. The closer the predicted values are to the actual values, the higher the degree of relationship between the two groups of values. If the ability to predict one variable from another were perfect, there would be no difference between the predicted and actual values, and all points would lie on a straight line. The standard error of estimate would be zero in this case. Then, as the standard error of estimate approached zero, the better the prediction and the more related the two variables. This measure, however, is influenced by the means and standard deviations of the samples. With any given standard error of estimate, the magnitude of relationship is not readily apparent. To be useful, a measure of relationship must have universal application. The interpretation must be the same in all cases. This may be accomplished by making the measure independent of means and standard deviations and by imposing some limits on the range of the statistic. Practitioners first tried to accomplish this by constructing a ratio of the form $\mathrm{SD}_{Y \bullet X}/\mathrm{SD}_{Y}$

There was still difficulty in interpretation because, as the ratio decreased toward zero, the relationship of the variables increased in magnitude. Finally, the measure took the form

$$r = 1 - SD^2_{Y \bullet X}/SD^2_Y$$

where r is the correlation coefficient. This defines the limits as $+1$ and -1 so that it is possible to have a single measure of the relationship of two variables which is comparable across sets of groups. A great advantage of this measure, the correlation coefficient, is that inverse relationships can also be described. An inverse relationship occurs when one variable increases in value as the other decreases. The following chart is a rough guide to the interpretation of correlation coefficients.

r	-1.00	$-.99$ to $-.80$	$-.75$ to $-.50$
interpretation of degree of correlation	perfect inverse relationship	high inverse relationship	moderate inverse relationship

r	$-.40$ to $-.25$	$-.20$ to $-.10$	0.00
interpretation of degree correlation	low inverse relationship	very low inverse relationship	no correlation

r	$+.10$ to $+.20$	$+.25$ to $+.40$	$+.50$ to $+.75$
interpretation of degree correlation	very low relationship	low relationship	moderate relationship

r	$+.80$ to $+.99$	$+1.00$
interpretation of degree of correlation	high relationship	perfect positive relationship

There are several ways to calculate r. All are based on abstract reasoning. The method one uses to calculate r is based on the information one has at hand. If z-scores are available, r may be found by the formula

$$r = z_X z_Y /n$$

If only raw scores are available, the covariation formula may be used:

$$r = \frac{\Sigma(X - \overline{X})(Y - \overline{Y})}{\sqrt{\Sigma(X - \overline{X})^2} \sqrt{\Sigma(Y - \overline{Y})^2}}$$

Probably the simplest formula to use when a calculator or computer is available is as follows:

$$r = \frac{\Sigma XY - (\Sigma X)(\Sigma Y)/n}{\sqrt{\Sigma X^2 - (\Sigma X)^2/n} \sqrt{\Sigma Y^2 - (\Sigma Y)^2/n}}$$

Each of the four computation methods described above has been used to calculate r for the test scores cited earlier in the chapter.

$$r = \sqrt{1 - \frac{SD^2_{Y \bullet X}}{SD^2_Y}}$$

$$= \sqrt{1 - \frac{(5.49343)^2}{(22.002)^2}}$$

$$= \sqrt{1 - \frac{30.1778}{484.088}}$$

$$= \sqrt{1 - .0623395}$$

$$= \sqrt{.93766}$$

$$= .968328 = .97$$

Test Scores

	A (X)	B (Y)	z_X	z_Y	$z_X z_Y$
	42	46	- .197093	- .0409054	.00806
	45	51	- .0671414	.186347	- .01251
	73	84	1.14574	1.68621	1.93188
	91	84	1.92544	1.68621	3.24661
	27	32	- .846848	- .677211	.5735
	63	55	.71255	.368148	.26233
	24	19	- .976799	-1.26807	1.23868
	81	85	1.49227	1.73166	2.58422
	53	51	.279395	.186347	.05207
	87	79	1.75217	1.45896	2.55646
	10	14	-1.58324	-1.49532	2.36736
	23	27	-1.02012	- .904463	.92264
	36	29	- .456995	- .813562	.3718
	64	61	.755882	.640851	.48441
	57	47	.192761	- .00454504	- .000877
	38	41	- .370361	- .268157	.09932
	27	29	- .846848	- .813562	.68896
	14	18	-1.40997	-1.31352	1.85204
	45	51	- .0671414	.186347	- .01251
	37	35	- .413678	- .54086	.22374
$\Sigma =$	931	938	0.00	0.00	19.4382
$\overline{X} =$	46.55	46.9			
$SD =$	23.0856	22.002			

$$r = \frac{\Sigma z_X \, z_Y}{n}$$

$$= \frac{19.4382}{20} = .97191 = .97$$

$$r = \frac{\Sigma (X - \overline{X})(Y - \overline{Y})}{\sqrt{\Sigma (X - \overline{X})^2} \; \sqrt{\Sigma (Y - \overline{Y})^2}}$$

$$= \frac{9869.54}{\sqrt{10658.9} \; \sqrt{9681.8}}$$

$$= \frac{9869.54}{(103.242)(98.3961)}$$

$$= .97154 = .97$$

$$r = \frac{\Sigma XY - \dfrac{\Sigma X \, \Sigma Y}{n}}{\sqrt{\Sigma X^2 - \dfrac{(\Sigma X)^2}{n}} \; \sqrt{\Sigma Y^2 - \dfrac{(\Sigma Y)^2}{n}}}$$

$$= \frac{53539 - \dfrac{(931)(938)}{20}}{\sqrt{53997 - \dfrac{(931)^2}{20}} \; \sqrt{53674 - \dfrac{(938)^2}{20}}}$$

$$= \frac{53539 - 43663.9}{\sqrt{53997 - \dfrac{866761}{20}} \; \sqrt{53674 - \dfrac{879844}{20}}}$$

$$= \frac{9875.1}{\sqrt{10658.9} \; \sqrt{96818}} = \frac{9875.1}{(103.242)(98.3961)}$$

$$= \frac{9875.1}{10158.6} = .97209 = .97$$

One must be careful in interpreting any measure of correlation. The best motto to follow is, "Correlation does not imply causation." To prove that one variable causes another is a long, involved, difficult undertatking. Correlation is a measure of relationship and nothing more.

Only the Pearson product-moment correlation coefficient, or r, has been discussed so far. This is the most common correlation coefficient and is used with test scores because the data collected most often meet the required assumptions. These assumptions are as follows:

1. Data must be continuous. Only interval-scale, ratio-scale, or absolute-scale measurements may be used to collect both variables. Test scores are assumed to be continuous.
2. Data must be approximately linear. This means that the line of

best fit would be straight, not curved, as the case would be when the data were grouped in a circle or U-shape.

3. Variance must be approximately homoscedastic. The points around the line of best fit must take on a uniform appearance. Along the regression line, the width of the pattern must be approximately equal from one end of the line to the other.

If these conditions are not met, another correlation coefficient could be used. Other coefficients are the Spearman ρ (rho), Kendall τ (tau), Kendall coefficient of concordance, point biserial, biserial, ϕ (phi), tetrachoric, and η (eta). Discussion of these is beyond the scope of this text.

Reliability

Reliability may be thought of as consistency of measurement. If approximately the same score is obtained every time an individual attempts a test instrument, the test is said to be reliable. For example, a child who earns a score of 105 on an IQ test would earn a score close to 105 upon repeated administrations, if the test were reliable.

There are four ways to determine reliability. Each will be discussed.

Test-retest. This is also called self-correlation. The same test is given twice to the same group and the scores obtained by each person on the first test are correlated with scores obtained on the second administration. The correlation coefficient of the sample is the test-retest reliability or index of stability.

A test is expected to yield consistent results even if there is some change in the conditions of testing or of the examinee. Changes in lighting, temperature, weather, health, fatigue, stress, and examiner rapport are examples of changes in conditions. Probably the most crucial variable is time itself. If the test-retest interval is too long, maturation of the child may be introduced as a variable. If the testing interval is too short, the effects of practice may interfere. A reliable test is expected to overcome these factors to a great extent, but it is generally unrealistic to expect stability of the reliability coefficient outside the retest range of a few hours to six months or so. The interval should be reported in the test manual if the test-retest method is used.

Because there are so many variables which may intervene between test administrations, many test makers prefer to use another method of determining reliability in which they have more control of the environment. With the test-retest method, reliability tends to be slightly underestimated.

Alternate-forms. In the alternate-forms method, the test author constructs two equivalent tests. Each must measure the same trait or skill. The first form is given to a sample of children and, at a future time, the second form is administered. Each child's first form score is compared to his second form score. With this method, the test constructor attempts to reduce the effects of practice (by using different items) and the effects of maturation (by using a shorter time interval between test administrations).

If both tests are administered on the same occasion, the effects of time are not being taken into account. Again, the interval should be reported in the manual. The most important consideration is whether the forms are truly equivalent. Test forms are equivalent when each has the same number of items; the item difficulty, format, and time limits are comparable; and the differences between any other factors such as content, administration, and physical layout are minimized.

When there is a time interval between administration of the equivalent forms, the alternate-forms method is considered the best measure of reliability. In general, there may be four sources of error in testing. These are: (1) stability of results over short periods of time may vary due to problems in test administration, (2) stability of results over short periods of time may vary due to changes in pupil characteristics caused by maturation or instruction, (3) the representativeness of the test items may be faulty (i.e., there may not be an adequate number of items to test a particular skill), and (4) different scores may be obtained when more than one person is asked to score a test, resulting from ambiguity of scoring instructions. The alternate-forms method with a time interval between administrations is the only method that measures the first three sources of error.

Split-half. This is also called the coefficient of internal consistency. In this method, a test is given only once, and half the test is compared with the other half. It has been found that the first half could not be compared with the second half of a test because effects such as fatigue and item difficulty combined to yield an inaccurate reliability coefficient. In some cases, the odd items are compared with the even items. This is sometimes not considered appropriate because it is a less powerful indicator. With the odd-even split, the number of test items is reduced by half. If a 100-question test were given, only 50 items could be used for each test. This is detrimental because, usually, the greater the number of items on each test, the greater the reliability. This problem led to the development of a correction formula called the Spearman-Brown formula, and it estimates the reliability as if each half were composed of the total number of test items. This is more efficient than constructing a test twice as long. The formula is as follows:

$$r' = 2r/(1 + r)$$

where r' is the estimated reliability and r is the reliability calculated from the two halves.

Other formulas have been devised which mathematically compare the correlation coefficients from all possible combinations of a test. Several formulas have been developed by Kuder and Richardson (e.g., KR-20, KR-21); and Cronbach devised a method called coefficient a (alpha). In general, these formulas tend to underestimate reliability slightly.

Split-half reliability measures are not appropriate for timed tests (also called speeded tests) unless the time allowed is so generous as to not be a factor at all. With timed tests, the reliability coeffcient tends to be inflated. Another problem with split-half methods is that a test's ability to reduce differences resulting from day-to-day performance is not taken into consideration.

Scorer reliability. Some tests, including measures of personality and creativity, demand a great deal of interpretation on the part of the scorer. When test results are dependent upon scorer judgment, a measure of scorer reliability should be reported. A set of tests should be given to two scorers and each should score all tests in the set. Then the two scores obtained on each test should be compared through calculation of a correlation coefficient. This coefficient would be a measure of the reliability of scorers. When scoring directions are ambiguous, this reliability should be reported.

Authors have commented on the reliability coefficients which should be obtained with various types of test instruments. Some feel that tests with coefficients of .9 or above are necessary when important educational decisions are being made. Others believe that achievement tests should have reliability coefficients of .9 or above, intelligence tests .85 or above, and other tests used in education about .8 or above.

Standard Error of Measurement

All tests contain error. Because of this error, the score earned on a test is not necessarily the true score. A true score may be estimated according to the formula

$$X' = \overline{X} + r(X - \overline{X})$$

where X' is the estimated true score, X is the mean of the test, r is the reliability coefficient calculated by the test-retest, alternate-form, or split-half methods, and X is the obtained score. This estimated true score is still subject to error. The best that can be done is to calculate a range of scores in which it is probable that the true score lies. To do this, the estimated true score, reliability, and standard deviation of a test must be used to calculate the standard error of measurement (SEM), and a confidence interval around the estimated true score must be constructed.

The SEM is calculated according to the following formula:

$$SEM = SD \sqrt{1-r}.$$

SEM may be thought of as the standard deviation of the curve of error around any particular score. By using the SEM, a distribution around the estimated true score may be constructed which captures the true score. The picture looks like this:

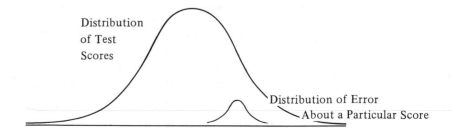

Distribution
of Test
Scores

Distribution of Error
About a Particular Score

The true score is expressed in terms of a confidence interval or range in which the true score lies. Because the SEM is a standard deviation and the area between +1 and −1 standard deviation of a normal curve contains 68 percent of the area, a confidence interval in which there is 68 percent certainty of capturing the true score would have a range of X' − SEM to X' + SEM.

As an illustration, assume that a child obtains a score of 105 on an IQ test with a mean of 100, a standard deviation of 15, and a reliability co-efficient of .92, the calculations for establishing confidence intervals would be as follows:

$$X' = \overline{X} + r(X - \overline{X})$$
$$= 100 + .92\,(105 - 100) = 100 + .92\,(5)$$
$$= 100 + 4.60 = 104.6$$
$$= 105$$

$$\text{SEM} = \text{SD}\,\sqrt{1 - r}$$
$$= 15\,\sqrt{1 - .92} = 15\,\sqrt{.08}$$
$$= 15\,(.282843) = 4.2426$$
$$= 4$$

Then, to be 68-percent sure that the true score is captured, the range would be

$X' \pm$ SEM or 105 ± 4 or 101 to 109.

If one wanted to eliminate most doubt that the true score was captured, ±2 standard deviations around the estimated true score would be used. The 96-percent level of confidence lies between 97 (105 − 4 − 4) and 113 (105 + 4 + 4). To be virtually "absolutely" sure of capturing the true score, use the 99-percent level of confidence or ±3 standard deviations from the estimated true score. With 99-percent certainty, it could be said that the child's true IQ score lies between 93 (105 − 4 − 4 − 4) and 117 (105 + 4 + 4 + 4).

Obviously, the smaller the SEM, the narrower the range of the confidence interval and the more precise the test. Following is an illustration of a test with high reliability and one with low reliability. In each, the 68-percent level of confidence is depicted.

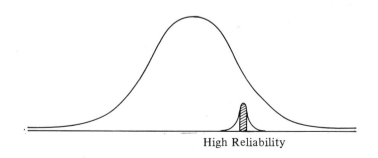

High Reliability

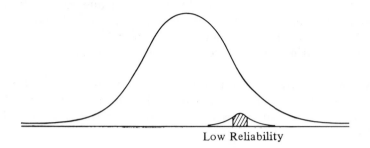

Low Reliability

Problems

The following problems are offered for the reader's practice.

1. Find the estimated true score when the obtained score is 85, the mean is 100, and the reliability coefficient is .84.
2. Find the SEM in the above problem when the standard deviation is 16.
3. In the above problems, what is the confidence interval for 96-percent certainty?
4. A child's score on an IQ test is 75. The test has a mean of 100, a standard deviation of 24, and split-half reliability of .91. Discuss this child's eligibility for special education services (MR or LD) based on this incomplete data.

Answers

1. The formula for the estimated true score is

    $$X' = \overline{X} + r(X - \overline{X})$$
    $$= 100 + .84(85 - 100)$$
    $$= 100 + (-12.6) = 87.4$$
    $$= 87$$

2. The formula for the SEM is

    $$SEM = SD \sqrt{1 - r}$$
    $$= 16 \sqrt{1 - .84}$$
    $$= 16 \sqrt{.16} = 16(.4) = 6.4$$
    $$= 6$$

3. The 96-percent level of confidence encompasses two standard deviations from the mean in either direction. The confidence interval is 87 ± 2 SEM or 75 to 99.
4. The first step is to calculate a confidence interval.

$$X' = \overline{X} + r(X - \overline{X})$$
$$= 100 + .91(75 - 100)$$
$$= 100 + (-22.75) = 77.25 = 77$$

$$\text{SEM} = \text{SD} \sqrt{1 - r}$$
$$= 24 \sqrt{1 - .91}$$
$$= 24 \sqrt{.09} = 24(.3) = 7.2$$
$$= 7$$

The 68-percent level of confidence band is 70 to 84. At the 96-percent level of confidence, the band is 63 to 91. With this information it is not possible to classify the child as MR, LD, or normal. The range of scores is too great and other evidence must be presented.

REFERENCES

Ebel, R. L. 1972. *Essentials of educational measurement.* Englewood Cliffs, New Jersey: Prentice-Hall.

Edwards, A. L. 1967. *Statistical methods,* 2nd ed. New York: Holt, Rinehart, and Winston.

Gronlund, N. E. 1971. *Measurement and evaluation in teaching,* 2nd ed. New York: Macmillan.

Lindquist, E. F. 1938. *A first course in statistics.* Boston: Houghton-Mifflin.

McNemar, Q. 1962. *Psychological statistics,* 3rd ed. New York: John Wiley.

Mills, F. 1955. *Statisitical methods,* 3rd ed. New York: Holt.

Noll, V. H., and Scannell, D. P. 1972. *Introduction to educational measurement,* 3rd ed. Boston: Houghton-Mifflin.

Schmidt, M. 1975. *Understanding and using statistics: basic concepts.* Lexinton, Massachusetts: D. C. Heath.

CHAPTER 9

VALIDITY

Reliability is a factor in validity. A test may be reliable and still not be valid; however, to be valid, a test must be reliable. Validity may be defined as the degree to which a test measures what its authors or users claim it measures and is probably the most important measure of the usability of a test. If only one factor is to be considered in judging a test, validity is the only choice. Validity involves a comparison of test performance with some other independent measure of the trait or skill in question.

There are three types of acceptable validities in use. Some combination of these should be reported in the manual of every standardized test. The ideal situation exists when each type of validity study is fully reported in the manual. Each type will be discussed in turn.

Content Validity

Content validity has also been called curricular validity. In considering a test, questions of the following arise:

1. Does the test measure what has been taught?
2. Does the test include a representative sample of items reflecting the skill to be measured?
3. If the skill is other than rote memory, does the test go beyond to tap understanding of the skill in question?
4. Have clues been eliminated which would allow correct responses to be chosen without having mastery of the skill being measured?

If the answer to all these questions is yes, the test is said to have content validity. The degree of content validity, however, cannot be precisely determined because there is no way to quantify content validity. There is no mathematical formula or statistical procedure available. Expert judgment is used in lieu of a more objective method.

This is accomplished through careful examination of test content. In the ideal situation, the test authors construct a table of specifications as the texts, objectives, scope-and-sequence charts, domains of learning, and child being measured. As the authors construct each test item, it is compared with the requirements set forth in the table of specifications for appropriateness. Then, when the test is completed, judges take it and evaluate the table of specifications itself and then determine how well the test items achieve the objectives set out in the table of specifications. To construct or evaluate a test instrument, it is necessary to do a thorough examination of curricula, texts, objectives, scope-and-sequence charts, domains of learning, and child development in the area being tested.

Included in the realm of content validity is an assessment of how well the format contributes to the validity of the test. If those taking the test were not familiar with the format used, the validity of the instrument might be questioned. Examples of typical formats include multiple-choice, analogy, true-false, and essay.

There is no numerical way to describe content validity, although some descriptive statistics may be employed in the evaluation. For each item of a test, the percentage of children obtaining a correct answer should be reported by grade or age. An item would be highly suspect if a greater percentage of, say, ten-year-olds than twelve-year-olds gained a correct answer. Applied to the whole test, one would question the fact that a group of fourth-graders obtained higher raw score totals than a group of fifth-graders.

Content validity seems most appropriate when applied to achievement testing because it is assumed that those being tested have had roughly the same academic experiences and that there exists a core of experiences from which to draw. In other types of testing, such as personality or creativity, there is no common pool of experiences; it is illogical to assume that most people go through the same set of experiences. One should expect to see a review of content validity in achievement and intelligence test manuals, but not necessarily for measures of less curricular orientation.

Probably the greatest difficulty with content validity, aside from the fact that there is no one numerical indicator, is that a consideration of the processes of reasoning used to arrive at answers is not generally included. Different reasoning processes applied to the same problem may lead to different answers. This question is addressed by construct validity.

There is a pseudo-type of validity, called face validity. It is often confused with content validity and may be described as an extremely superficial form of content validity. The question to be asked is, "Does the instrument appear valid on its face?" Stated differently, the question is, "By quick inspection, does this test appear valid?" Often, face validity is reported through testimonials of its users. If content, criterion-related, and construct validity are fully discussed in the manual, testimonials may give an indication of a test's ease of administration, scoring, interpretation, and whether or not the format is motivating to the persons being tested. Statements of face validity, however, should never be accepted uncritically and are not substitutes for validation reports.

Criterion-related Validity

Criterion-related validity is also called statistical or empirical validity. If a good measure of the skill to be tested exists, it is possible to compare that measure with the score obtained in the test being constructed. This is achieved through the use of the Pearson product-moment correlation coefficient. The measures which may be correlated with a test include other tests, ratings, grades, length of service in a particular position, yearly income, and clinical judgment.

Two types of criterion-related validity exist. They are concurrent and predictive. Each will be discussed in turn.

Concurrent validity asks if a test score can be used to predict present performance. In this case the question becomes one of asking if current performance on an independent criterion measure could be estimated through administration of the test under consideration. A specific example is in order. Assume that a test maker wanted to show that his test was an accurate estimator of reading comprehension. He would gather a sample of students and determine at what grade level each was functioning in the reading comprehension strand of the reading curriculum. The easiest way to do this is to ask the teachers of the students. After administering the test and calculating the estimated grade levels, the test maker would compare the score of each student from the test with the grade level reported by the teacher as taken from the reading comprehension strand of the reading curriculum. The correlation coefficient obtained would be a measure of the test's concurrent validity.

Another example has to do with intelligence testing. Assume that a student earns a certain score on an IQ test. What guarantee is there that the score is valid (i.e., that this test is really measuring intelligence)? It is common in both IQ and achievement testing to compare a group of student scores on a test with their scores on another test which has been shown to be valid. In intelligence tests, the most common standard of comparison is the *Stanford-Binet Intelligence Test.* If the correlation between an IQ test and the Stanford-Binet is high, it is assumed that strong evidence of concurrent criterion-related validity has been demonstrated. This is an essential consideration if IQ test scores are to be used for placement purposes.

Several sources of error may be cited. Comparing test scores with grade levels from curriculum will not yield a fair validity coefficient if the curriculum in question is not similar to the curriculum being used with the students in question. In intelligence and achievement testing, there are great numbers of subareas. Only a relatively small sample can be presented on a test. If that sample is not representative of what the students have experienced, then the validity will be artificially lowered because the test is not tapping student experience.

With ratings, grades, and clinical judgment, subjectivity is a consideration. Because a dependance on subjectivity generally yields somewhat less reliable scores, the validity obtained from comparing these measures with a test instrument must be expected to be lower.

If a test is used as the standard of comparison which has questionable validity, the validity of the test in question may be affected. In 1954 the first widely accepted set of standards for constructing tests was disseminated. The Joint Commitee of the American Psychological Association, American Education Research Association, and National Council on Measurement in Education has published a set of standards which was an expanded version of the 1954 standards. The latest revision was published in 1974. Because many tests have been constructed before these standards came into widespread acceptance, the criteria for test construction have not been met for many of the tests which are now on the market.

Authors have proposed various cut-off points for acceptable validity coefficients. When intelligence test scores are correlated with other test scores purporting to measure the same traits, the validity coefficient probably should not be less than 0.60 and is not likely to be greater than 0.85. Achievement tests used for important decisions should probably have validation coefficients no lower than .80 when compared with other tests. If test scores are correlated with other criterion measures, the coefficients will generally be lower.

Predictive validity is differentiated from concurrent validity by time. Where concurrent validity estimates performance on another measure administered at the same time, predictive validity is used as a measure of performance on another criterion at a later date. While criteria such as graduation or job success clearly belong in the realm of predictive validity, performance next week or next month on a related measure could appropriately be placed in either category, depending on circumstances. There are no universally accepted guidelines separating concurrent from predictive validity along a continuum of time. For this reason, the differentiation between concurrent and predictive validity is becoming less distinct.

Construct Validity

Construct validity can be referred to as logical validity. In the validation of most tests, it is essential that both construct and criterion-related validity studies be reported in the test manual. If for some reason this information cannot be obtained, a report of construct validity should be included in the manual. It is most beneficial if all three types of validity studies are reported.

Construct validity is an attempt to answer the question of how well a test measures a theory or trait or construct. For example, there are several theories about intelligence. One proposes that there is a general trait called intelligence, another poses a number of equally weighted factors, while others weight factors such as memory or reasoning ability differently than manual dexterity or visual perception. With construct validation, the test maker attempts to show that her test does in fact measure those factors proposed in a theoretical orientation. This is accomplished through indirect evidence and inference. Empirical evidence is marshalled to support the contention that a test has construct validity.

As an example, a general statement is that skills increase with age. If a test has construct validity, raw scores should increase as a function of age (i.e., older students should get higher raw scores). Another factor to be considered is correlation with other types of tests. Different types of tests should not correlate well. An intelligence test should not correlate well with a motor proficiency test, for example. If the correlation is high, then there is evidence that the two could be measuring the same construct. This is not the intent of the tests. It is thought that, say, intelligence and motor proficiency are different traits, although some feel that motor ability is a factor in intelligence. Moderate correlations can be expected if that is the case. This does not mean that high correlation is assurance that two tests are measuring the same trait. Remember that correlation is not causation and that high correlation may result from an outside intervening variable. The high correlation is often nothing more than an indication of coincidence.

A relatively new technique has been applied to the examination of traits or constructs. It is called factor analysis and is used most successfully with computers. With this kind of program, computers are able to group similar traits into clusters which, when analyzed, give testers indications of the elements included in constructs. With this as a basis for research, theoretical constructs should lend themselves more easily to validation research.

Some test authors report internal consistency studies as indices of construct validity. Strictly speaking, unless it is demonstrated that a link exists between internal consistency and a theoretical construct, internal consistency is simply a measure of split-half reliability and nothing more. Be wary if a test manual is unclear in its explanation of internal consistency.

Quantifying construct validity is quite difficult because there are a number of diverse factors involved. A coefficient reported may represent one of several factors. There could be multiple coefficients reported, but there is no way to combine these into a single summative coefficient.

Validity covers a great deal. To show validity, it is necessary to demonstrate that a number of conditions have been fulfilled. In light of its wide range and complexity, a substantial amount of space in the test manual should be devoted to the methods in which the particular test was validated.

REFERENCES

Anastasi, A. 1976. *Psychological testing,* 4th ed. New York: Macmillan.

Miller, D. M. 1972. *Interpreting test scores.* New York: John Wiley.

Noll, V. H., and Scannell, D. P. 1972. *Introduction to educational measurement,* 3rd ed. Boston: Houghton-Mifflin.

Salvia, J., and Ysseldyke, J. E. 1981. *Assessment in special and remedial education,* 2nd ed. Boston: Houghton-Mifflin.

CHAPTER 10

STANDARDIZATION AND NORMS

Almost every teacher has received the results of formal tests and felt that the profile developed from test results did not reflect the child's classroom performance. Years of experience told the teacher that the child's functioning was not captured by the test instruments.

A number of factors could be cited which would explain this seeming discrepancy between predicted and actual achievement. The student may develop high anxiety or confidence during tests and earn significantly different scores than expected. The reliability and validity of the test or tests may not meet the guidelines as presented in Chapters 8 and 9. If that is the case, the test results should be questioned. If the reliability and validity are satisfactory, standardization factors should be checked.

Standardization

Standardization can be defined as the process of eliminating ambiguity in the administration, scoring, and interpretation of tests. The test manual should include clear directions for the administration of the test. For each child who takes the test, the directions should be presented in an identical manner. Standardization means that each person taking the test does so under the same conditions. In addition to correct directions, there are other factors to check. Was the room comfortable? Was the lighting bright enough, but not glaring? Did the examiner establish good rapport with those being tested? Were the correct time limits observed, if any? Did those tested appear to be ill, upset, or fatigued? Were the correct forms and levels of the tests used? Any deviation from the standards established in the manual is a potential source of error. When this occurs, there is a strong possibility of obtaining incorrect scores.

Several problems may arise in scoring. The most embarrassing is when the examiner's countings or computations are not correct. One must double-check all addition, subtraction, multiplication, and division involved in obtaining a score. It is also imperative to make sure that all raw scores have been correctly recorded. One of the easiest errors to make is to record a raw score in the blank next to the subtest and then mistakenly record a different numeral elsewhere on the test protocol. Raw scores must often be transferred to a separate page before calculations are begun. A check must be made to insure that the correct scores are recorded in the correct blanks. It is also necessary to make sure that the correct tables were used and that they were used correctly. Credit can be incorrectly given. Directions in the manual should be very clear about scoring procedures. Many tests have nonstandard procedures for scoring. As an example of this, on some tests, a student may score zero raw score points, yet still be awarded standard score points. One thing which may be excessively troubling is interpolation and extrapolation. Interpolation is the calculation of an unknown score between two given scores, and extrapolation is the calculation of an unknown score beyond two given scores.

Norms

Correct interpretation of results may be somewhat difficult. The question to be asked is, "What does a particular score mean?" To answer this question, many people look at a particular score in relation to the norms established for the test. Norms may be defined as the average test performance of the standardization sample. These are established empirically. A representative group called the standardization sample is exposed to the test instrument and the group average score and standard deviation is thought to represent those of the population. The range of average may be statistically defined as the scores lying between +1 and −1 standard deviations from the mean. At this point the test maker attempts to change the quantified data into qualitative information by attaching labels to score ranges. These labels can be inaccurate for several reasons.

One reason for inaccurate labels may be that the sample obtained is not really representative of the population as a whole. A relatively small group is used to standardize a test because it is not possible either to test each person in the population or even to test a very large percentage of the population. The time and effort involved would be exhorbitant. There is an assumption that the relatively small sample mirrors or captures the range of traits or characteristics of the population, but this may not always be true. If there is a mismatch between population and sample, then the scores obtained will either underestimate or overestimate the quantity of the trait in question. A grievous mismatch may yield extremely distorted scores and much error in the labels applied to the persons taking the test.

For example, tests have been standardized on a sample consisting of children from only the northeastern part of the country, or white middle-class children in an urban setting in the southeast, or nonhandicapped public school children. If a teacher ran, say, a resource room for mildly handicapped children in a rural area of the southwest part of the country, the characteristics of children in the class would probably not be comparable to the standardization samples mentioned because each group might have had a different set of educational and socialization experiences.

Another source of error may occur when the children being tested have characteristics or experiences quite different from the population as a whole and when the labels obtained from testing are used in a punitive manner. Some learning disabled children, for example, may earn lower and lower verbal IQ scores as they grow older because they fall farther and farther behind and profit less and less from the educational experiences available. It is this kind of circumstance which may lead to an incorrect placement in a class for the retarded. Similarly, those whose subculture is different from the norm may find themselves being treated differently than others, even though they function normally within their environment.

In either case, the examiner should look for a different test instrument. One hopes that he will be able to find one in which the experiences of the standardization sample are either closer to those of the population as a whole or closer to those of the children in class. Failing that, the examiner may want to inquire about the establishment of local norms.

Local Norms and National Norms

In the search for another test, an examiner will look at the manuals carefully. After consideration to determine if the stated purpose of the test matches the objectives for testing, she will pay close attention to reliability and validity data and then will look at standardization data. Is the sample used completely described in terms of age, grade level, sex, region, degree of urbanity, socioeconomic status (SES), race or ethnicity, type of community, ability level, and acculturation of parents? The examiner is suspicious if there isn't an attempt to gather a sample which has the same proportions in each of the just-listed characteristics as the population. This is most easily done through reference to United States census data. It is also necessary to have a large enough sample so that infrequent characteristics can be represented in the sample. At least 100 subjects per age or grade level should be included in the sample. It is desirable to include at least 200 subjects in each age or grade level.

The examiner also checks the manuals for other factors which are important in testing, such as ease of administration, time of administration, preparation time, ease of scoring, and difficulty of score interpretation. After all these factors have been considered, a decision must be made. At this point, the experiences of the students may not adequately be represented in the tests reviewed. If so, it is possible to take the original test and establish a set of local norms for use with the students. The same process to establish the local norms as the test makers used to establish their set of norms may be used. This makes sense because the same type of information is gained from either national or local norms (i.e., how a given child ranks in relation to his peers). A review of the norming process is in order.

Establishing Norms

Before norms can be established, it is necessary to develop a test instrument. Here the examiner already has an instrument, but still looks at the process of test construction because he is interested in making sure that the instruments used to affect a student's future are fair. Most standardized tests take several years to develop. Several steps are involved. The authors should work from a plan in which several statements are made, including the purpose of the test, content and constructs to be measured, age and grade levels for which the test is intended, length of proposed administration time, number of parallel forms to be built, and types of items to be used. When this is done, a number of test items should be written and the number of specified forms constructed. At this time, a small sample is given the test and the results are analyzed in terms of item discrimination and difficulty. Discrimination is the ability to separate the knowledgable from the less competent student on the trait being measured, and difficulty of an item is considered fair when about fifty percent of the sample population answer it correctly. The final forms of the test instrument come out of this analysis. Only after these steps are completed can the test be normed and the manual written.

Gathering a sample is usually thought of as the first step in the establishment of norms. Test makers should try to make this sample as representative of the population as a whole as possible by using census data and sophisticated sampling procedures. With local norms, the size of the school community often dictates procedure. In a small system, data should be collected for several years. Remember, a minimum of one hundred students per grade level should be tested for purposes of establishing norms. In a middle-size system, perhaps it is possible to use all children in each grade level in a given year. This is quite convenient because it is not so time consuming as waiting several years to collect data and does not force one to deal with the problems in cutting down the sample size. In a large system, a fraction of the students in one year form the norm sample. Here some system for insuring the generation of a random sample must be instituted.

Scores are gathered by age level or grade level for analysis. Usually grade level is preferred because the age range within each grade level is sometimes quite wide. The test may be given, for example, in February to fourth-grade students. Their average raw score is considered to be the average raw score for fourth-grade students in February. If the average raw score was, say, 315, then subsequent test takers scoring 315 would be said to be at grade level 4.6 (February is the sixth month of the school year.) Standard deviation in raw score points is also calculated so that standard scores may be figured. This is done because it is too confusing to talk in terms of raw scores. With a common ground for discussion such as standard scores, a child's score may be compared across tests.

The same process is followed for each of the other grade levels or age levels. Many test makers include both a table of percentile scores and stanine scores for convenience in converting raw scores into scores of relative standing.

The process of norming is completed when any gaps in age or grade levels are closed through interpolation or extrapolation. It is convenient if the test maker performs these calculations.

At this point, the examiner may be wondering if all the effort and cost necessary to establish local norms makes the process worthwhile. Each of the following five factors should be considered.

1. Local norms give an indication of the performance of children who should have been exposed to roughly the same set of experiences. With this information it may be possible to adapt curricula or recommend methods and materials which would enhance the instructional program. Since the same instrument is being used in both cases (national and local norming), however, and since the rankings of indivividual children are not usually changed by using local norms, it appears that an item analysis may be of more use than a different norming procedure. In an item analysis, the performance of a child or class or district on each item of the test is scrutinized. Because there is an assumption that several curricula are involved in a nationally standardized test, there will be relatively few items which are representative of any one type of curriculum (such as modern math or functional English). It might be wise, therefore, to take this information and combine it with the results gained from criterion- or mastery-testing to address the question of how good are the curriculum, methods, and materials in use.

2. Local norms may yield a very different picture in terms of average performance. For example, if the average raw score for grade 4.6 is 83 for a national sample and 67 for a local sample, this does not necessarily mean that the school district is inferior to other districts. One interpretation is that the activities stressed or the opportunities provided in the instructional milieu of that district are quite different. The task then becomes one of finding an instrument which will assess the skills stressed in the local curriculum. When this is done, both the instruction provided in the district and the ability of students are checked. It must be kept in mind that, if students leave the district or apply for postsecondary school training, their performance will most probably be judged on national norms.

3. An analysis of national norms in several skill areas has shown that several variables may affect an individual's score. Different regions yield different mean scores. Also, children from the same socioeconomic categories tend to have similar scores. Girls as a group tend to score differently than boys. Some test makers think these sex differences are important enough to justify separate norm tables for boys and girls. With this in mind, local norms

might be useful so that a more realistic set of expectations can be developed. For example, if children from a high income suburban district are earning scores close to the mean for their age or grade level, that might be cause for alarm. Similarly, if children in a depressed urban district are earning high scores, one might want to pay close attention to the instructional atmosphere in effect so that others could benefit. Again, one would not necessarily have to establish local norms to gain this information, but it would be necessary to collect data so that it could be compared with the national norms.

4. Local norms are sometimes used to predict success in certain courses (e.g., Biology II or English literature) or programs within a district (e.g., college prep, honors, vocational education, special education). The use of local norms over national norms does not change the rank order positions of pupils with respect to each other. If one has a program in which there are 16 openings and 25 candidates, it is irrelevant whether national or local norms are used. It may be important to establish cut-off points, but this can be done independently of norm considerations.

5. National norms should be used for traits not related to individual school districts. Examples are intelligence tests and college entrance examinations. This is because intelligence and college success are related to level of development, and the standard of comparison is the national population. The question is one of how an individual functions rather than an assessment of that individual's potential. From this, an indication of how a person will do may be inferred, but this is usually on the basis of cut-off scores.

Each district has different needs. Keeping the options open and using the options appropriately are the best guarantees that students will be served in the most efficacious manner.

REFERENCES

Anastasi, A. 1976. *Psychological testing,* 4th ed. New York: Macmillan.

Green, J. A. 1970. *Introduction to measurement and evaluation.* New York: Dodd, Mead.

Gronlund, N. E. 1971. *Measurement and evaluation in teaching,* 2nd ed. New York: Macmillan.

Noll, V. H., and Scannell, D. P. 1972. *Introduction to educational measurement,* 3rd ed. Boston: Houghton-Mifflin.

Salvia, J., and Ysseldyke, J. E. 1981. *Assessment in special and remedial education,* 2nd ed. Boston: Houghton-Mifflin.

Womer, F. B. 1965. *Test norms.* Reston, Virginia: National Association of Secondary School Principals.

CHAPTER 11

INTERPRETING TESTS
AND TEST REPORTS

Before test interpretation is performed, it is a good idea to review the testing process to make sure that the most appropriate tests were used for the situation at hand. Tests are one part of the assessment package, but are an extremely important part of that package. Information gained from testing is dependent on the appropriate use of test instruments, the quality of the test instruments, and the ability of the examiner to administer normed tests under standardized conditions. Because they are important in the educational assessment process, it is imperative that the most accurate, most useful information be obtained from tests. The futures of children may depend on it.

Instrument Accuracy

A number of factors should be considered in judging the usefulness of a test or test battery. It is necessary to make sure a test or battery has been chosen to investigate the problem at hand. For example, an educationally relevant problem statement is that Johnny seems to be significantly behind in arithmetic. The examiner then can choose an instrument or battery which will help to confirm this statement and also investigate the specific problems Johnny is experiencing, so that remedial help may be given. Before any testing beyond screening is performed, a mission or purpose must be understood. The examiner must know why each instrument is being administered. With this in mind, it should be much easier to choose a test or battery to address the specific problem. This procedure should also lead to less overtesting and the subsequent needless duplication of information.

When referrals are written, special education placement is always a possibility. Testing should be performed, first, in the areas of intelligence and achievement. If the results suggest a possibility of exceptionality, testing in adaptive behavior may be in order. Again, specific reasons must be at least tacitly understood before testing. Instruments are matched to the needs of children based upon the characteristics of the children being tested. The process is not one in which the examiner chooses tests as a result of her familiarity with them, or their ready availability, or because all children must be given a certain test battery.

There are thousands of tests on the market today. Even experienced examiners must continually search for the most appropriate instruments for given situations. Good sources of information include the *Mental Measurements Yearbook* (Buros), test reviews in journals and texts, dicussions with colleagues, publishers' catalogs, and test manuals.

A number of points should be kept in mind when selecting a test.

1. What is to be measured? In the example of arithmetic problems just cited, the examiner is interested in providing some insight into what is causing Johnny to fall behind and if there is a strategy or strategies which will help Johnny to catch up with his classmates. Intelligence testing is also performed in order to see what potential Johnny is bringing to the situation. In the event that indicators of handicap appear, adaptive behavior could then be measured. It would be even better to have more specific information on arithmetic difficulty and a listing of other symptoms which Johnny is exhibiting in class.
2. Why measure this behavior? Johnny is perceived by his teacher to be falling behind his classmates to an alarming degree. The possibility of special education placement exists and legal mandates are very specific in their documentation requirements. Aside from the legal realm, testing is performed to help Johnny achieve at a higher level in arithmetic.
3. How should this behavior be measured? There are several ways to collect samples of behavior for evaluation. This text is primarily concerned with the understanding of the statistical components of testing. It is assumed that formal tests will be used to obtain a measure of Johnny's arithmetic and intellectual capabilities. Before any test is used, there are a number of factors which should be checked.

Validity. Does each test measure what it says it measures? This is checked through validity studies which should be done by the test makers and reported in the test manuals. There are three kinds of validity and all are interrelated.

Content validity is a check by experts to see if the test items meet the design specifications set forth by the test authors. No statistics are involved. A judgmental statement about content validity should be included in the test manual. This is especially important for intelligence and achievement tests.

Construct validity is a determination of the extent to which the test measures the theory or trait or construct in question. If intelligence is thought to be, say, eye-hand coordination or the texture of one's hair, then a test should measure the various aspects of eye-hand coordination or the texture of hair. Until recently, it was necessary to rely solely upon the judgment of clinicians in determining the construct validity of a test. At present, a relatively new statistical technique called factor analysis is being increasingly used. Most test manuals will not yet report information of this nature, however.

Criterion-related validity is divided into concurrent validity and predictive validity. Concurrent validity is a correlation in which results of the test in question are compared with the results of another measure taken at the same time. Predictive validity correlates results from the test in question with a future measure. For intelligence tests, the coefficient of correlation should be no less than .60; for achievement tests, the coefficient should be no lower than .80 if the tests will be used for the purposes of placement. Validity is probably the most important single measure of a test's usefulness. A more complete discussion is presented in Chapter 9.

Reliability. Is the test capable of giving stable scores over a period of time? If Johnny took the same arithmetic achievement test twice over a two-week period, he should be expected to earn scores which are quite close. If so, the test is probably reliable. In the event Johnny scored at a 3.2 grade level the first time he took the test and at 1.1 grade level the second time, it would be quite difficult to make educational decisions unless the discrepancy in scores could be attributed to external factors such as health, an emotional block, or whatever. A reliable test will yield about the same score for the same individual over a period of time. Reliability may be tested in three ways. Test-retest reliability is obtained by calculating the correlation coefficient from the same test given at two different times to the same sample. Split-half reliability uses a single sitting, and one-half of the test is correlated with the other half. Equivalent-forms reliability occurs when two separate forms of the test are given at different times to the same sample and the results correlated. Reliability coefficients for achievement tests ideally should be no less than about .90. For intelligence, the coefficient should probably be no less than .85. For personality, the ideal coefficient should be no less than .70 or .80. Chapter 8 contains a discussion of reliability.

Standardization. Standardized testing means that each person taking the test does so under the same conditions. These include time limits if any, directions, temperature, lighting, health, rapport, noise level, seating comfort, and scoring. No one should be given advantages or burdened with disadvantages from external sources. Standardization is discussed in Chapter 10.

Norms. Was the test adequately normed? A test should have at least one hundred subjects per age or grade level in the standardization sample. The sample should also be representative of the population in terms of age, socioeconomic status, and other demographic variables. The test should have been normed on a sample which included characteristics of the person being tested. Another important consideration is that the person being tested should fall within the age range upon which the test was normed. Chapter 10 contains a discussion of test norms.

Administration. Is the test easy to administer? Some tests require extensive preparation—directions must be memorized; theoretical interpretations must be made during the testing; and the examiner must be familiar with a complicated test format. Some tests are easier to score than others. Some tests take less time to give and interpret than others. Some include a high cost for the amount of information obtained. If the validity, reliability, and norms of two or more tests are comparable, the examiner should choose the test to be used on the basis of ease of administration.

Error. All tests contain error. Several sources are possible. Internal error lies within the instrument itself. This type of error is calculated as the standard error of measurement and is a function of the reliability of the instrument. It is desirable to use a test with the lowest possible standard error of measurement. A confidence interval is constructed around a score through use of the standard error of measurement. The lower the standard error of measurement, the smaller the range of the confidence interval and the more precise the test score. A more complete discussion of the standard error of measurement appears in Chapter 8.

External error may appear when the conditions of administration are not duplicated—temperature, lighting, noise level, seating, rapport, health, and scoring. Scores may be incorrectly transferred from the subtests to the scoring section of the test protocol. There may be computational errors. Tables may be read incorrectly. A score may be graphed incorrectly. It is a good idea to triple check all scoring.

Each of the above factors should be checked before initiating test interpretation. The elimination of inaccurate information should lead to a lower incidence of prejudgment on the part of the test interpreter.

Test Interpretation

As each test is administered, the examiner asks if the information gained suggests other areas to be tested. Once the test information is gathered, it must be interpreted. This is performed with individual tests, and then a composite profile is obtained by assessing all information collected—formal and informal tests, anecdotal records, ratings, clinical judgements, etc.

Many tests allow the examiner to report scores in several forms. These include percentiles, standard scores, stanines, and age and/or grade scores. With this information, a label may be attached to the data. Cut-off points may have been established by the test constructor or others. In the past, the assigning of a label ended the diagnostic process for all practical purposes. Because the emphasis has shifted from labeling to giving meaningful educational help, it is necessary to use the test information as part of the prescriptive effort. Questions the examiner must keep in mind include: "What can and can not the child do educationally?" "What are the causes of the problems?" "What will help educationally?" The examiner must check the results of tests to see if data from one test supports data collected on other tests. The tester asks what each score means, if it is supported by other data, and what methods, materials, and curriculum will help the child in question.

The examiner may have to perform an item analysis to determine error patterns. Although common error patterns exist, remedial strategies must be individually determined. No direct, one-to-one relationship exists between a child's test scores and the best specific educational programming available. Children bring too many educationally relevant variables to the test situation and classroom for that. In fact, some of the broader assumptions about test performance which seemed to be "cast in concrete" are now being challenged. For example, even the pattern of low verbal, high performance scores on tests of intelligence as an indicator of learning diabilitiy is being questioned (Dudley-Marling, Kaufman, and Tarver 1981). Extensive experience with both children and testing is necessary to provide the most efficient help necessary to support training.

The Test Report

A diagnostic report brings together all the information collected about a child for the purpose of providing the child with the best educational programming possible. Formal testing is an important part of that bank of information. A good report relates the areas of referral information, test information, and prescriptive recommendations. In this way a "feel" for the child and his problems is gained. If anything in the child's background is directly related to his educational problems, it should be stated. The diagnostic report is a good place to make a statement about the child's modality preference or modality difficulty. Learning style may be indicated, as well as a preferred teaching style, if any. Attitude toward learning, if significant, should be mentioned.

A statement of how the child functions in each of the areas tested is necessary. A composite picture should emerge from the testing, including an indication if the various traits or symptoms displayed may be grouped into educationally relevant syndromes. Strategies for educational programming may be discussed. This information should be used to construct a statement of recommendations which are stated as specifically as possible.

Any reported information should be understandable to its consumers. Obscure or extermely technical terms must be avoided unless defined for the reader. Chapter 12 will show how the report process is accomplished through an examination of two of the reports presented in Chapter 1. An outline of the process follows.

Outline for Judging Tests and Test Reports

Tests
What is to be measured?
Why should this behavior be measured?
How should this behavior be measured?
Formal tests:
check validity
check reliability
check standardization
check norms

check administration
check for error—internal (SEM) and external

Test Interpretation
  Are the scores reported in several forms?
  What can the child do in the area tested?
  What discrepancies exist?
  What does the test suggest educationally?
  Is other testing in order?

Test Report
  Has all test information been integrated?
  Is this an accurate educational picture of the child?
  Are the recommendations relevant?
  Are the recommendations specific?
  Are the recommendations practical?
  Are data clearly presented?

REFERENCES

American Psychological Association, American Educational Research Association, and National Council on Measurement in Education. 1974. *Standards for educational and psychological tests.* Washington, D. C.: American Psychological Association.

Buros, O. K. (ed.). 1978. *Eighth mental measurements yearbook.* Highland Park, New Jersey: Gryphon Press.

Dudley-Marling, C., Kaufman, N., and Tarver, S. 1981. WISC and WISC-R profiles of learning disabled children: a review. *Learning Disability Quarterly* 4:3 pp. 307-319.

Miller, D. M. 1972. *Interpreting test scores.* New York: John Wiley.

Noll, V. H., and Scannell, D. P. 1972. *Introduction to educational measurement,* 3rd ed. Boston: Houghton-Mifflin.

Salvia, J., and Ysseldyke, J. E. 1981. *Assessment in special and remedial education,* 2nd ed. Boston: Houghton-Mifflin.

Turnbull, A. P., Strickland, B. B., and Brantley, J. C. 1978. *Developing and implementing individual education programs.* Columbus, Ohio: Charles E. Merrill.

Vodola, T. M. 1974. *Descriptive statistics made easy for the classroom teacher.* Bloomfield, New Jersey: C. F. Wood.

CHAPTER 12

TWO TEST REPORTS

The test report or psychological report is one source of data in the placement process. In light of its importance, extreme care must be taken to insure accuracy. In Chapter 11, an outline was presented which can be used to
judge the test report. When that process is completed, other information is
combined with that report to produce a label. If the child in question is
found to be handicapped, an IEP should be written, followed by a placement
decision. This chapter will exemplify the process of judging test reports with
two of the students presented in Chapter 1—Audri and George. Please review
those test reports. Chapter 13 will carry the process of evaluation through an
IEP to a placement decision for one of the students—Audri.

AUDRI

Some very specific educational problems were reported in writing
skills, phonics, and memory. Five formal tests were administered. An analysis of each will be presented, followed by a critique of the test report as a
whole.

WISC-R

This is one of the most widely used and respected IQ tests.
Technical aspects.
Validity: There are limited data reported in the manual, but all cri-

terion-related coefficients are at least .60. These coefficients fall above the acceptable minimum for an IQ test.

Reliability: Overall split-half reliability coefficients are at least .90 for Verbal IQ, Performance IQ, and Full-scale IQ. At Audri's age (CA 8 years 6 months), these coefficients are .92, .91, and .95, respectively. Reliability is judged to be quite good.

Standardization: The manual states that 200 children per age level were used in the standardization sample and chosen to be representative of the population on the basis of age, sex, geographic area (four regions), occupation of head of household, and urban/rural residence. Standardization is judged to be very good.

Norms: Three types of scores are available—standard scores (deviation IQ scores), scaled scores, and percentile ranks. IQ scores outside the range of 40 to 160 cannot be determined. As with other IQ tests, it is more difficult to determine accurate IQ scores as one scores farther from the mean.

Administration: This test can only be given after extensive supervised training. Interpretation of subtests requires clinical judgment. In comparison with other individually administered IQ tests, this one is easier to administer than many for the quality of information obtained.

Error: At Audri's age (CA 8-6), the standard error of measurement, expressed in IQ units, for Verbal, Performance, and Full Scale scores is 3.86, 4.48, and 3.23, respectively. This is good for an IQ test. Although complicated, scoring is made easier by the clear directions found in the manual.

Test Interpretation. In this report, the subtest scores are not reported in any form. This is a clear deficiency. Verbal, Performance, and Full Scale scores place Audri within the normal range of intelligence. An indication is given that Audri is significantly below average in Vocabulary (defining words), Comprehension (understanding verbal directions and social mores), Digit Span (immediate recall of several series of orally presented digits), Picture Arrangement (sequencing pictures to make a story), and Coding (copying symbols on paper). Average scores on subtests are generally thought to lie between +1 and −1 standard deviations from the mean. Without scores, it is not possible to determine if the examiner is using that convention.

Some grouping of subtest deficiencies was done to confirm the referral problems of following directions, using phonics, and remembering the alphabet. The possibility of reading problems was raised. It would have been better, however, to dwell more on what specific skills Audri exhibited or failed to exhibit in the various subtests. It is tacitly understood that the results suggest achievement and perceptual testing.

WRAT

This achievement test is used for screening and clinical purposes.
Technical aspects.
Validity: No content validation is reported in the manual. For an achievement test, this is surprising and a matter for concern. In the 1978 edition, criterion-related studies seem inadequate and, in some cases, mislead-

ing. The test must be used with caution.

Reliability: The manual does not fully report the studies. All split-half coefficients are above .90. In Audri's age range (five to eleven years), Reading is .98, Spelling is .96, and Arithmetic is .94.

Standardization: No attempt was made to obtain a representative standardization sample.

Norms: A number of scores are available—grade ratings, scaled scores, stanines, *T*-scores, and percentiles. These are available from preschool to adult.

Administration: Very easy administration is a great strength of this test. Teachers find it quite attractive because little preparation time is required, scoring is easy, and the test is relatively inexpensive to purchase.

Error: Incomplete reliability data makes judging the internal error somewhat difficult. The standard error of measurement appears quite good. It is not reported in the manual in what units the standard error of measurement is expressed. In Audri's age range (five to eleven years) the standard errors of measurement are: Reading, 1.05 to 1.39; Spelling, .86 to 1.20; and Arithmetic, .88 to 1.42. External error is minimized through the ease of administration of the instrument.

Test interpretation. The examiner reported the scores in three forms—percentile, grade level, and standard score. Audri is just barely in the normal range in Reading (recognizing capital letters, naming capital letters, and saying words in isolation). This lends some support to the limited vocabulary problem reported in the referral information. No mention was made in the test report of phonics ability or alphabet problems. Spelling (skills in copying marks on paper, writing one's name, writing single words from dictation) is below average. No comments with regard to left-to-right tracking behavior or alphabet memory were noted. Although no question involving arithmetic skills was noted in the referral information, Audri scored below average in Arithmetic (counting, reading numerals, solving orally presented problems, performing written computation of arithmetic problems). The interpretation of the results of this test ignores some pertinent referral problems. A consumer of this information has the right to question its completeness.

Woodcock Reading Mastery

This reading achievement test is designed for K-12 use.

Technical aspects.

Validity: Content validity appears good. Construct validity was demonstrated through the use of a sophisticated statistical technique. Criterion-related validity has not been well established. Predictive validity to many readers will appear to be an alternate-forms reliability study.

Reliability: Two problems are apparent. The Letter Identification subtest is not very reliable, especially at older age levels. Also, the reliability at older age levels is lower than at younger age levels. Audri is young enough that the only problem might lie with the Letter Identification subtest. At grade level 2.9, the total test reliability is .99 for split-half reliability and .97

for test-retest reliability. This is excellent.

Standardization: The process was well explained and it appears that a very representative sample was obtained.

Norms: Grade scores, mastery scores, and percentiles are available.

Administration: This is difficult at first until familiarity is gained with the instrument. Scoring is lengthy and complicated.

Error: Standard error of measurement is reported in raw scores and mastery scale scores. A standard error of measurement of 5.0 in raw scores at grade level 2.9 with a mean of 173.6 and a standard deviation of 50.3 is quite good. External error in the form of clerical mistakes may be a problem. The analogy format of some subtests seems to disturb some children and it is possible that a depressed score results. Familiarity with that format is a good idea before the test is administered. This will help insure that content and not format is being tested.

Test interpretation. In the report on Audri, virtually no information of substance is presented to the reader. In this case, the administration of this test appears to have been a waste of time.

KeyMath Diagnostic Arithmatic Test

This arithmetic achievement test has clinical applications.

Technical aspects.

Validity: Content validity appears to be good. Criterion-related validity has not been completely established.

Reliability: Split-half reliability is reported for each grade level from K to 7. The test has good reliability as shown by the .94 to .97 range of coefficients.

Standardization: This is incomplete. A representative sample was not obtained and only part of the test was administered to each child in the sample.

Norms: Only raw scores and grade scores are available. This is a serious deficiency of this test.

Administration: A good description in the test manual and good directions make this an easy test to administer and score. The test has clinical applications.

Error: Standard error of measurement is expressed in raw score units and this makes it difficult to obtain confidence intervals. The test is constructed to minimize errors.

Test interpretation. The real strength of this test lies in its use as a clinical instrument. Here, this has not been done. No analysis of Audri's arithmetic behavior has been attempted. The reader does not have an indication of what the child can and cannot do in arithmetic, nor an idea of where to start the informal testing process. Little value has been gained from the administration of this test.

Illinois Test of Psycholinguistic Abilities (ITPA)

This test of psycholinguistic ability has generated a great deal of discussion.

Technical aspects.

Validity: No studies have been reported in the manual or supplementary material by the authors. The consumer is not assured that the test is actually measuring psycholinguistic abilities.

Reliability: Internal consistency studies yielded coefficients from .87 to .93, and the coefficients from test-retest studies were between .70 and .83. These are somewhat lower than expected for an instrument of this type.

Standardization: The sample selected is not representative of the population at large.

Norms: A number of scores are available—scaled scores, psycholinguistic age, and psycholinguistic quotient. Audri is within the normed age range.

Administration: Extensive supervised practice is necessary before one can administer and interpret this test. Clinical judgment is required.

Error: Standard error of measurement units are reported for raw scores, scaled scores, and psycholinguistic age scores. At Audri's age, the composite scaled score standard error of measurement is 1.9 with a mean of 36 and a standard deviation of 6. One must exercise caution in interpreting test scores. As a result of its clinical nature, room for interpretive error exists. Clerical errors are possible.

Test interpretation.

No interpretation is done in this report beyond the confirmation of auditory channel and memory problems. The examiner failed to tap a collection of information rich in useful data.

Test Report

A great deal of data were collected, but not enough interpretation was performed. The examiner did integrate the data to the extent that an auditory memory hypothesis was proposed; WISC-R data were used to substantiate several conclusions; and the discrepancy in arithmetic scores among three of the tests was noted. Even so, the picture presented is less than complete. Audri's referral problems have not been fully addressed. A comprehensive picture of Audri's strengths and weaknesses was not provided. Not enough justification for learning disability placement is apparent. Recommendations are stated in such general terms as to preclude educational relevance. A teacher would label these as superficial and question the credibility of the report writer. The examiner appears to be more of a technician than clinician. With more effort, the examiner could have delivered to the consumer a more educationally meaningful summary of Audri's performance.

GEORGE

Language arts and reading are the areas in which George is experiencing difficulty. It appears that these problems are related to general low academic achievement. The referral information is somewhat sketchy. In George's case, a more comprehensive test battery is warranted.

Stanford-Binet

This may be the most widely respected IQ test in use.

Technical aspects.

Validity: No validity data are reported in the manual for the 1972 edition. The 1960 edition relied to a great extent on data gathered for the 1937 edition.

Reliability: No data are reported for the 1972 edition. The reliability of the 1960 edition is based on the 1937 edition data.

Standardization: Although approximately 100 individuals were tested at each age level, the manual for the 1972 edition does not describe the demographic characteristics of the sample. As a result of the way in which it was gathered, the sample may not have been representative of the population.

Norms: A mental age (MA) and deviation IQ are available. This test is widely used for low functioning children.

Administration: This test can only be given after extensive supervised training. It is very difficult to administer and score.

Error: Standard error of measurement is not reported in the manual for the 1972 edition. Clerical errors are possible. A great strength of the instrument is its clinical usefulness. This can also be a liability if, as in this case, the test demands ongoing scoring, much manipulation of material, and some degree of clinical judgment as the test is being administered.

Test interpretation. Because this was previous testing, no interpretation was included in the current report. The value of the score lies in its historical significance.

WISC-R

This instrument has been evaluated in the previous report.

Technical aspects. At George's age (CA 14 years 6 months), split-half reliability coefficients for Verbal IQ, Performance IQ, and Full Scale IQ are .95, .89, and .96, respectively. The standard errors of measurement, expressed in IQ units, for Verbal IQ, Performance IQ, and Full Scale IQ are 3.40, 4.74, and 3.15, respectively.

Test interpretation. In this report the scores are very well reported. George's high average functioning is highlighted by his above-average scores in Picture Completion (identifying missing parts in pictures) and Block Design (reproducing a design with blocks). The examiner hypothesizes that George has good visual, visual-motor, and visualization skills, but some problem with auditory skills. Because no scores are significantly low, George has the ability to cope with the normal classroom. Possible motivation problems must be considered.

The *Stanford-Binet* and WISC-R are two of the most widely used and respected IQ tests. The *Stanford-Binet* was given five years before the current WISC-R. In a study done with the two tests and reported in the WISC-R manual, it was found that at ages 6, 9-6, and 12-6, students who took both tests scored about two IQ points higher on the *Stanford-Binet*. Given this information, it can be seen that George's performance on the *Stanford-Binet* in 1976 would be roughly equivalent to a WISC-R score of 113. His current WISC-R score of 110 is equivalent to the 1976 *Stanford-Binet* score of 115 when the standard error of measurement is taken into consideration.

WRAT

This test was reviewed in the previous report.

Technical aspects. In George's age range (12 to 24 years), split-half reliability coefficients are .98 for Reading, .97 for Spelling, and .94 for Arithmetic. Standard error of measurement is reported as 1.33 to 1.70 for Reading, 1.13 to 1.34 for Spelling, and 1.21 to 1.38 for Arithmetic.

Test interpretation. Scores are well reported. George scored in the average range in Reading and significantly below average in Spelling and Arithmetic. This seems contrary to the referral information. The Reading subtest, however, is pronunciation of words and does not involve comprehension. It was hypothesized that Spelling scores may have been adversely affected by handwriting and motivation problems. Arithmetic problems have not been discussed.

Woodcock Reading Mastery

This test was reviewed in the previous report.

Technical aspects. Only two of the five subtests were administered. The split-half reliability of the Word Identification subtest at grade 10.9 is .97, and the reliability for the Word Attack subtest is .94. Raw score standard error of measurement units are 1.9 and 2.1, respectively. Subtest coefficients are normally lower than whole test coefficients. It is encouraging to note the high reliability of these subtests.

Test interpretation. A good way to individualize the test battery is to use subtests of a test instrument. Diagnostic information can sometimes be gathered very efficiently and used clinically. In this case, one must wonder why the Word Identification subtest was administered. Its similarity to the Reading subtest of the WRAT seems to make this a duplication of effort. The Word Attack subtest is a quick test of phonetic ability. Results of this confirm the fact that George is having trouble with phonics, but still falls within the normal range.

KeyMath Diagnostic Arithmetic Test

This test was reviewed in the previous report.

Technical aspects. The test was normed on a sample of children from grades K through 7. Results obtained from an older student should be interpreted with caution. The test yields clinically useful data.

Test interpretation. An indication of strengths and weaknesses is given, but the list is not specific as to competencies demonstrated. The examiner has not presented hypotheses to explain the scores.

Auditory Discrimination Test

This is a commonly used test (most people call it the Wepman) to determine the ability to differentiate among sounds.

Technical aspects.

Validity: Data are incompletely reported. In one study, the *Auditory Discrimination Test* scores were correlated with each subtest of the Metropolitan Achievement Test. Coefficients ranged from .24 to .35. This is below recommended values.

Reliability: Test-retest reliability was reported in the manual as .91 in one study and .95 in another. This is an indication of good reliability.

Standardization: No report is given in the manual.

Norms: The test was evidently normed on children aged 5 to 8. A raw score and five-point qualitative rating scale are available.

Administration: This is a quick and easy test to give. Scoring at first is slightly confusing. Raw scores are converted to a five-point rating scale. It is not clear how the examiner obtained a quotient of 118. No mention of quotients is made in the manual.

Error: Standard error of measurement is not reported in the manual. External error is minimized by the simplicity of administration.

Test interpretation. Because this test apparently was normed for use with five to eight-year olds, any score obtained on a child outside that range is questionable. The scoring system is somewhat crude for a normed test. As a clinical device, the test has some use. However, a number of sounds are not included. It may be possible to obtain much of the information through clinical use of the Word Attack subtest of the Woodcock.

Bender Visual-Motor Gestalt Test

This instrument is used as a test of visual-motor perception, emotional adjustment and personality, brain damage, and sometimes as a rough measure of intelligence. Nine geometric designs are reproduced by the examinee.

Technical aspects. At least five scoring systems are available (Bender, 1968; Hutt, 1969; Koppitz, 1964; Clawson, 1962; and Watkins, 1976). Many public school personnel use the Koppitz scoring system. It is assumed that this system was used by George's examiner.

Validity: Construct validation seems to be lacking. In concurrent criterion-referenced studies, *Bender* scores were correlated with intelligence and achievement scores. At ages five and six, the correlation coefficients between the *Bender* and the *Stanford-Binet* were .79 and .63, respectively. At ages seven, eight, nine, and ten, the coefficients between the *Bender* and WISC were .61, .48, .54, and .59, respectively. Correlation with the *Metropolitan Achievement Test* was .68, with the *Lee-Clark Reading Readiness Test* .61, and the *Metropolitan Readiness Test* .59.

Reliability: Two types are reported. Interscorer reliability studies were done because of the subjective nature of the test. Most of these coefficients were above .90. Test-retest coefficients ranged from .50 to .90 and are somewhat lower than expected for a test which may play a prominent part in placement decisions.

Standardization: Demographic characteristics of the population were not matched by the sample, and the sample sizes for each age range are not equal.

Norms: A mental age called a perceptual age or developmental age is available. At several age levels, the mean raw score is exceeded by the standard deviation.

Administration: This test is very easy to administer. Scoring is somewhat subjective, but examples of expected drawings at various ages help considerably.

Error: Standard error of measurement is not reported. Subjective error is possible.

Test interpretation. After age ten, the test does not discriminate among students because virtually all normal children obtain perfect or nearly perfect scores. Evidence to support the test's ability to diagnose mental retardation, emotional disturbance, brain damage, learning disability, and visual perceptual problems is not very convincing. The test does not help in educational programming for individual children. Its strength lies in its use as a projective device. Combined with WISC-R data, there is some evidence to suggest motivational problems.

Draw-A-Person

This is one of several projective techniques in which the examinee is asked to draw a human figure or figures. The Urban manual was probably used. Goodenough (1926), Machover (1949), Jolles (1952), Harris (1963), Buck (1964), and Silver (1983) have developed this type of test.

Technical aspects.

Validity: Comparatively less research has been done in this area.

Reliability: Various research has shown both that children's drawings are quite variable from one administration to the next and also that children's drawings are somewhat consistent from one administration to the next. Interscorer reliability studies yield similar conclusions.

Standardization: None of these tests appears to meet the guidelines specified for a representative sample.

Norms: The test may be used from age five through adult. A mental age based on detail recognition may be obtained. There is a 16-item Severe Mental/Emotional Disturbance Checklist and a 14-item Organic Brain Damage Checklist. Much of the information is qualitative, although other authors provide standard scores, IQs, and percentile ranks. Urban died before presenting evidence of the efficacy of his scoring system.

Administration: The student is asked to draw a person. Scoring is highly subjective.

Error: The two greatest sources of error are that the examiner may project his own personality into the student drawings and that the drawings may be evaluated on the basis of student artistic ability.

Test interpretation. George's figure is comparable to that of a twelve-year-old. Other information gathered from this test is not discussed. The reader must assume that brain damage is not indicated. Validity of this test has not been adequately established and the findings must be interpreted with caution.

Detroit Tests of Learning Aptitude (DTLA)

This test is often used with children beyond the age range of the ITPA.

Technical aspects.

Validity: This has not been adequately stated in the manual. Apparently there was a criterion-related study with an IQ test, but coefficients are not stated.

Reliability: Two test-retest studies are reported in the manual. After a five-month interval, the correlation coefficient was .959. After a two- to three-year interval, the correlation coefficient was .675. The first study yielded good reliability; results of the second have been affected by the relatively long time between administration.

Standardization: Fifty children at each age level were taken from the Detroit Public Schools. An IQ of 90 to 110 obtained on group intelligence tests was a criterion for inclusion in the sample. This type of sample is woefully inadequate.

Norms: The test may be used from age five through adult. A mental overall IQ may be calculated.

Administration: Between nine and thirteen subtests should be administered. Each one tests a different quality, and many formats are used. The test is not difficult to administer and score.

Error: Standard error of measurement is not stated in the manual, but has been reported as eight IQ points in the literature. Some subjective interpretation must be made.

Test interpretation. This test if often used to demonstrate perceptual deficits. Auditory problems are indicated, but it is difficult to know to what extent these are affecting George's performance. Lack of more types of scores and the questionable validity of this test make interpretation difficult.

Test Report

George shows the type of intelligence score pattern not often typical of a learning disabled individual. Often, on verbally loaded tests such as the *Stanford-Binet* and WISC-R Verbal IQ, over time the IQ will drop. This may be interpreted as an increasing failure to deal with the symbolic aspect of language with consequent failure to keep up academically. In George's case, this has not happened.

Mental retardation is immediately ruled out on the basis of George's IQ scores. Emotional disturbance is not warranted as a diagnosis because there is no indication that George's behavior is sufficiently severe, offensive, and chronic to be significantly deviant.

Although George could legally qualify for special education services at this point, he probably is not learning disabled. Uncorrected vision problems and motivation problems are apparent. His academic problems could be mitigated by a change in educational programming. If George could experience some success in his academic endeavors, his motivation might be improved. Recommendations are well stated and justified.

REFERENCES

Baker, H. J., and Leland, B. 1967. *Detroit tests of learning aptitude,* rev. ed. Indianapolis: Bobbs-Merrill.

Bender, L. 1968. *A visual-motor gestalt test and its clinical use.* New York: American Orthopsychiatric Association Research Monograph no. 3.

Buck, J. 1964. *House-tree-person: administration and interpretation of H-T-P test.* Los Angeles: Western Psychological Services.

Clawson, A. 1962. *Bender visual-motor gestalt test for children.* Los Angeles: Western Psychological Services.

Connolly, A. J., Nachman, W., and Pritchett, E. M. 1970. *KeyMath diagnostic arithmetic test.* Circle Pines, Minnesota: American Guidance Service.

Durost, N. N., Bixler, N. H., Wrightstone, J. W., Prescott, G. A., and Balow, I. H. 1971. *Metropolitan achievement test.* New York: Harcourt Brace Jovanovich.

Goodenough, F. 1926. *Measurement of intelligence by drawings.* New York: World.

Harris, D. 1963. *Children's drawings as measures of intellectual maturity. New York: Harcourt, Brace, and World.*

Hildreth, G. 1946. *Metropolitan achievement test, primary 1 battery: form R.* Yonkers-on-Hudson, New York: World.

Hildreth, G., and Griffith, N. L. 1949. *Metropolitan readiness test.* Yonkers-on-Hudson, New York: World.

Hutt, M. 1969. *Hutt adaptation of the Bender gestalt test,* 2nd ed. New York: Grune and Stratton.

Jastak, J. F., and Jastak, S. R. 1978. *Wide range achievement test.* Wilmington, Delaware: Jastak Associates.

Jolles, I. 1952. *A catalogue for the qualitative interpretation of the H-T-P.*

Los Angeles: Western Psychological Services.

Kirk, S. A., McCarthy, J. J., and Kirk, W. D. 1968. *Illinois test of psycholinguistic abilities,* rev. ed. Urbana, Illinois: University of Illinois Press.

Koppitz, E. M. 1964. *Bender gestalt test for young children.* New York: Grune and Stratton.

Koppitz, E. M. 1975. *Bender gestalt test for young children: research and applications, 1963-1973.* New York: Grune and Stratton.

Lee, J., and Clark, W. 1962. *Lee-Clark reading readiness test.* Monterey, California: California Test Bureau.

Machover, K. 1949. *Personality projection in the drawing of the human figure.* Springfield, Illinois: Charles C Thomas.

Paraskevopoulos, J. N., and Kirk, S. A. 1969. *The development and psychometric characteristics of the revised Illinois test of psycholinguistic abilities.* Urbana: University of Illinois Press.

Silver, R. A., 1983. *The Silver drawing test of cognitive and creative skills.* Seattle: Special Child Publications.

Terman, L. M., and Merrill, M. A. 1937. *Measuring intelligence.* Boston: Houghton-Mifflin.

1960. *Stanford-Binet intelligence scale: manual for the third revision, form l-m.* Boston: Houghton-Mifflin.

1973. *Stanford-Binet intelligence scale: 1972 norms edition.* Boston: Houghton-Mifflin.

Urban, W. 1963. *Draw-a-person: a catalogue for interpretive analysis.* Los Angeles: Western Psychological Services.

Watkins, E. O. 1976. *The Watkins Bender-Gestalt Scoring System.* Novato, California: Academic Therapy.

Wechsler, D. 1949. *Wechsler intelligence scale for children.* New York: Psychological Corporation.

1974. *Wechsler intelligence scale for children—revised.* New York: Psychological Corporation.

Wepman, J. 1958. *Auditory discrimination test.* Chicago: Language Research Associates.

Woodcock, R. W. 1972. *Woodcock reading mastery tests.* Circle Pines, Minnesota: American Guidance Service.

CHAPTER 13

USING DATA TO CONSTRUCT AN IEP

Audri's educational problems have been discussed in Chapters 1 and 12. With this information in hand, it is possible to use informal testing to complete the initial evaluation process. Suggestions for individualized educational programming should become apparent as the testing is completed. It is especially important to have a grasp of Audri's capabilities in the basic skill areas of language arts and arithmetic.

Informal Testing

Writing problems were mentioned first in the referral information. A writing sample was collected. Audri was asked to write a simple four-sentence passage from dictation, to copy a twelve-sentence story, and to write a short composition. In each instance she wrote in manuscript rather than cursive form. It was found that *b* and *d* were occassionally reversed. There is evidence (Deno and Chiang 1979) to suggest that reversals are a learned cognitive skill and that a behaviorally based program may be quite effective in increasing the occurrence of correct responses.

In the dictation exercise, she had difficulty with spelling and forgot some of the words in each sentence. Her copying was slow and laborious. During this exercise, she did not follow the story line and could not answer questions regarding the main idea or details of the story. Her composition was short and choppy. Audri does not grasp the idea that writing is a tool for understanding and communicating meaning. Her writing needs to become more automatic and smoother. Much practice would help.

Audri was asked to write in cursive. After she stated that she was not "into cursive," she was asked to write the alphabet. Correct responses were: *a, b, c, e, g, h, i, j, k, m, n, o, p, t, u, x, y, B, C, H, J, M, N, O, T, U, V,* and *X.* Alphabet memory problems were noted in the referral information. When shown a cursive model of those letters she was not able to write, her attempts at copying produced large, poorly drawn letters. When asked to write the sentence, "He can pick a tomato," she connected only the *an* in *can,* the *pi* and *ck* of *pick,* and *om* of *tomato.* Practice in learning individual letters and connecting letters would help.

About one-quarter of the time, Audri would attempt to write from right to left. Perhaps some cueing device such as a green stripe down the left side of the page would improve her performance.

In phonics, the Woodcock was given, but the test protocol was not available. The Word Attack subtest was readministered as an informal measure. Analysis showed that consonant sounds were known. Vowel sounds were confused, but in an inconsistent manner. One time Audri would pronounce the short *e* as short *i;* the next time the short *e* might be pronounced as short *e* or short *i* or short *u.* Sound blending skills were not well developed. Audri has the capacity to differentiate among sounds, but has not yet learned vowel sound-symbol correspondence. Her approach suggests that she does not realize that word attack skills are a means to the end of understanding. Sound-symbol correspondence should precede development of sound blending skills.

Audri was asked to read a passage from a third grade reader. Poor phonics skills and an inadequate sight vocabulary made the going quite difficult. A beginning second grade reader was tried with better results. Audri could read approximately 95 percent of the words and answer 75 percent of the comprehension questions. When given a basic sight word test (Ekwall 1981), Audri named 65 of the 68 at the grade 2.5 level, 28 of the 60 at the 2.9 level, and 3 of the 15 at the 3.5 grade level. Apparently Audri needs a great deal of experience with a word before it becomes part of her vocabulary. Unless presented in isolation, new words seem to be confusing to her. When questioned, Audri admitted that she did not employ a rehearsal strategy to help in her memorization.

After a story at the fourth grade level was read to her, she answered verbally stated comprehension questions at the 75-percent level. In light of the formal test results, this was not expected. Audri said she liked stories because she didn't have to worry about learning and could just listen. Anxiety reduction must be considered in Audri's educational programming.

Arithmetic protocols were not available. Audri was given pages from second- and third-grade workbooks. Because little about arithmetic performance was reported in the assessment information, it was decided to concentrate on computational skills. Addition, subtraction, and multiplication problems were given to her. In addition, she counted on her fingers. One-digit plus or minus one-digit problems were solved by counting. Two-digit plus or minus one-digit problems were solved in an inconsistent manner. Audri would take the larger addend and count on her fingers the smaller addend to obtain the sum. She would take the minuend and count backwards the value of the subtrahend to find the difference. When asked to solve the problem without counting, she became confused and did not appear to know how to use the empty ten's place in the addend or subtrahend. When given two-digit plus two-digit problems, she stated that these were too hard for her unless she had her bundles of sticks. It was the examiner's impression that Audri did not use the algorithm to solve problems and relied solely on the concrete matching method. Even simple multiplication was beyond her reach. Audri knew the addition facts through three plus twelve and the subtraction facts through ten minus two. No multiplication facts were known.

When given story problems up to grade level three, she would often disregard relevant information and "invent" facts. This left her hopelessly confused. She could tell time to the half-hour, knew the value of coins and paper money, and was able to measure a book to the nearest inch.

Audri could follow orally stated one-step directions all of the time and two-step directions about two-thirds of the time. When given three-step directions, she would usually do the first step and state that she forgot the rest.

The IEP

This combination of formal and informal test data collected facilitates the construction of an individualized education program (IEP). Federal law mandates that a child's present educational performance levels, annual goals, instructional objectives, educational services, projected dates of such services, evaluation criteria, and extent of participation in regular education services be included in the IEP.

A sample IEP using the information collected about Audri follows:

IEP

NAME: Audri Green   **SEX:** F   **DATE:** 12/19/80
PARENTS: Mr. & Mrs. Samuel Green
ADDRESS:
TELEPHONE: **BIRTHDATE:** 5/24/72   **CA:** 8–7
SCHOOL: Walker   **GRADE:** 3
TEACHER(S): Rhoda Caspar

SIGNATURES OF APPROVAL:
Parents: Date:

Teacher(s):   Date:

School Representative: Date:

EDUCATIONAL CLASSIFICATION: Learning Disabled
SPECIAL EDUCATION PLACEMENT: LD Resource Room
INITIATION DATE: 1/5/81   **TERMINATION DATE:** 6/5/81
PARTICIPATION IN REGULAR PROGRAMS: 75%

RELATED SERVICES	PERSON RESPONSIBLE	AMOUNT OF TIME / %	INITIATION DATE	TERMINATION DATE
none				

CURRENT EDUCATIONAL PERFORMANCE

Aptitude: Audri scored in the normal range on the WISC–R, administered 11/11/80. Her verbal score was 91, Performance was 93, and Full Scale was 91. She has the ability to cope with the requirements of the regular class. Below average scores were earned on the subtests of Vocabulary, Comprehension, Digit Span, Picture Arrangement, and Coding. This pattern suggests that practice in memory skills is warranted and that remedial reading is indicated.

Reading: On the WRAT, Audri scored at the 19th percentile or grade level 2.4. On the Woodcock and informal reading measures, Audri read at a second grade level. This was consistent with her vocabulary. Her comprehension is erratic. In a more informal setting she was able to answer comprehension questions presented orally after a 4th grade level story was read to her. Anxiety may be hindering academic achievement.

Word Attack Skills: These are poorly developed. Audri pronounces the consonant sounds, but confuses vowel sounds. Sound blending skills are weak. Her sight word vocabulary is approximately that of a beginning second grader.

Writing Skills: These have been developed to approximately second grade level as measured by the Zaner-Bloser charts. In cursive, she was not able to produce: d, f, l, q, r, s, v, w, z, A, D, E, F, G, I, K, L, P, Q, R, S, W, and Z. Letters in words are connected approximately one-quarter of the time.

Spelling: On the WRAT, Audri scored at the 12th percentile or grade level 1.9. She took a great deal of time to print each letter in each word.

Arithmetic: On the WRAT, Audri scored at the 10th percentile or grade level 1.8. She is able to solve problems if she is able to use her fingers as counters. She knows her addition facts through three plus twelve and subtraction facts through twelve minus two. No multiplication facts were known. Story problems are confusing to her. She tells time to the half-hour, states the value of coins and paper money, and can measure objects to the nearest inch.

Other: Audri is able to follow orally presented one-step directions, has trouble with approximately one-third of a list of twelve two-step directions, and is able to follow the first step only of three-step directions. She remembers her address and telephone number after great difficulty and prefers to print when asked to write.

GOALS AND OBJECTIVES

Goal Area: Reading

Annual Goal: Audri will improve her reading ability in both vocabulary and comprehension from grade level 2.4 to 3.5 as demonstrated by an earned score on a standardized reading achievement test.

Objectives:

- After rehearsing an additional five words on flashcards each week for 20 weeks, Audri will state each word of the cumulative list when flashed until she states 90 words correctly.
- Given any vowel, Audri will say both its long and short sound with 100% accuracy.

- When presented with a list of 50 unknown words, Audri will blend the sounds of the letters of each word until she states the word, pronouncing 45 of the 50 correctly.
- Given five four-panel comic strips cut into panels and presented randomly, Audri will sequence four of these correctly.

Goal Area: Writing

Annual Goal: Audri will write in cursive at the average third grade level as modeled by the Zaner-Bloser charts.

Objectives:

- When asked to write, Audri will always start each line on the left hand side of the page.
- Given the letters *b* or *d*, Audri will print each without reversals with 100% accuracy.
- Upon command, Audri will write in cursive the letters d, f, l, q, r, s, v, w, and z, approximating the Zaner-Bloser model for the average third grader.
- Upon command, Audri will write in cursive the letters A, D, E, F, G, I, K, L, P, Q, R, S, W, and Z, approximating the Zaner-Bloser model for the average third grader.
- In cursive writing, Audri will connect the letters of each word with 100% accuracy.
- Audri will take dictation from a second grade text in reading at the average rate of 12 words per minute.

Goal Area: Spelling

Annual Goal: Audri will increase her spelling proficiency from grade level 1.9 to grade level 3.0 as measured by a standardized spelling test.

Objectives:

- Given five additional spelling words (three from second grade level and two from third grade level) each week, Audri will orally spell the cumulative list correctly from memory until she adds 50 words to her repertoire.
- Given any 10 of the spelling words above, Audri will write the words with correct spelling with 90% accuracy.

Goal Area: Arithmetic

Annual Goal: Audri will demonstrate achievement at the 3.1 grade level in arithmetic as measured by a standardized arithmetic test.

Objectives:

- Upon command, Audri will state the answers to any 10 addition facts randomly generated up to five plus twelve with 100% accuracy with each response occurring within two seconds after presentation.
- Upon command, Audri will state the answers to any 10 subtraction facts randomly generated up to twelve minus five with 100% accuracy with each response occurring within three seconds after presentation.
- Upon command, Audri will state the answers to any 10 multiplication facts randomly generated up to four times four with 100% accuracy within three seconds of each presentation.
- Given five story problems at the third grade level, Audri will state the relevant information and set up the correct computation with 80% accuracy.

— Given ten two-digit plus one-digit addition problems, Audri will write the answers to all within 30 seconds with 90% accuracy.

REFERENCES

Arena, J. 1976. *How to write an IEP.* Novato, California: Academic Therapy Publications.

Barbe, W., Lucas, H., Hackney, C., and McAllister, C. 1979. *Creative growth with handwriting,* 2nd ed. Columbus, Ohio: Zaner-Bloser.

Deno, S. L., and Chiang, B. 1979. An experimental analysis of the nature of reversal errors in children with severe learning disabilities. *Learning Disability Quarterly* 2:3 pp. 40-45.

Ekwall, E. E. 1981. *Locating and correcting reading difficulties,* 3rd ed. Columbus, Ohio: Charles E. Merrill.

Jastak, J. F., and Jastak, S. R. 1978. *Wide range achievement test.* Wilmington, Delaware: Jastak Associates.

Lerner, J. 1981. *Children with learning disabilities,* 3rd ed. Boston: Houghton-Mifflin.

Sloan, H. N., Buckholdt, D. R., Jenson, W. R., and Crandall, J. A. 1979. *Structured teaching.* Champaign, Illinois: Research Press.

Stellern, J., Vasa, S. F., and Little, J. 1976. *Introduction to diagnostic-prescriptive teaching and programming.* Glen Ridge, New Jersey: Exceptional Press.

Turnbull, A. P., Strickland, B. B., and Brantley, J. C. 1978. *Developing and implementing individual education programs.* Columbus, Ohio: Charles E. Merrill.

Wallace, G., and Larsen, S. C. 1978. *Educational assessment of learning problems: testing for teaching.* Boston: Allyn and Bacon.

Wechsler, D. 1974. *Wechsler intelligence scale for children—revised.* New York: Psychological Corporation.

Woodcock, R. W. 1972. *Woodcock reading mastery tests.* Circle Pines, Minnesota: American Guidance Service.

CHAPTER 14

TEACHERS AND PARENTS

Of all school personnel, parents deal most often with their child's teacher. Many times, a special relationship is developed in which parents place great faith in the teacher's ability. Parents may come to the point of establishing a relationship of trust such that the teacher enjoys the greatest credibility of all school personnel. When any programming is proposed, it is not unusual for the parents to consult with and follow the advice of the teacher. Parents may come to the teacher for an explanation of test results in plain English in a relaxed, nonthreatening atmosphere. The teacher's job is to make clear the child's present level of performance, discuss the implications of evaluation results, explain the available options, and give an indication of the prognosis of the child in question. Even after they consult a school psychologist, parents often wish to come to the teacher for confirmation and further explanation of their child's educational diagnosis.

By employing this special relationship with parents, teachers can greatly facilitate the process of establishing the best educational environment possible for all students. By gaining an understanding of the concepts presented in this text and consulting with the school psychologist and other school personnel, the teacher should be able to relieve parental anxieties by providing explanations which parents can understand. They may feel the need to consult the teacher at any time in the child's educational experience.

Parents come in different shapes and sizes, interests and abilities, and aptitudes and experiences. The sensitive teacher must adapt his explanation to the needs of the parents. No one explanation will be sufficient for parents, and the teacher must learn to explain the same data in several different ways. As an example, one explanation of the data collected about Audri will be presented. With this explanation as a basis, teachers can adjust their discussions so that parents can feel they were given a cogent, but not tedious, explanation. It is important that parents understand as much as possible of the academic and social progress of their child so that their participation in the educational process will be as meaningful as possible.

The information on Audri has been presented in Chapters 1, 12, and 13. Please review those chapters before reading the explanation below.

Explaining the Data

Chronologically presented explanations are often the easiest for the parents to understand. A good starting point is the referral information. Audri's teacher noticed that her educational performance was different than expected in several ways. It is not usual for children who are eight years old to still reverse their *b*s and *d*s in writing or to write occassionally from right to left. These problems will probably disappear with maturity and some instruction, but they are troublesome when seen in combination with Audri's other difficulties. Memory seems to be a problem. Audri apparently has trouble remembering alphabet letters, the sounds of the letters, sight words, and spoken directions. She has difficulty recalling words she wishes to use in speech. Part of her difficulty is caused by her failure to pay attention to what is important in class. This is not because she has a bad attitude. In fact, she is very cooperative and always tries hard to please. At times she is anxious to do well to the point that her anxiety hinders her learning.

Children who have difficulty with reading, writing, or arithmetic are a cause of great concern to the teacher. Audri got behind in these academic skills to the point that the teacher thought that extra help might be needed. Her learning pattern did not seem to be like that of the other children. At this point, Audri was referred for psychological testing.

A battery of tests designed to compare her aptitude and achievement with other children was given. These tests also were given in the hope that particular problems could be diagnosed so that the best possible instructional programming could be secured for Audri. First, the WISC-R was given. This IQ test was given to determine what could be expected of Audri in the classroom. She scored in the normal or average range, which indicates that she is capable of coping with the regular school curriculum. Many theories about intelligence exist. The test Audri was given divides intelligence into verbal ability and performance ability. Verbal ability is the ability to use the symbols of communication found in language and mathematics. Five or six types of verbal abilities are tested and the scores are used to obtain the Verbal IQ score. Performance ability is the mastery of designs and patterns to solve problems. Five or six types of performance abilities are tested and the scores are used to obtain the Performance IQ score. Then the Verbal IQ and Performance IQ are used to obtain the Full Scale IQ or total IQ score. IQ scores falling between 85 and 115 are normal or average. Audri scored in the normal range for all three scores.

Sometimes it is possible to gain an indication of problems by looking at the patterns of scores among the subtests. Children who have reading problems sometimes have a pattern similar to that of Audri's (i.e., low scores on the subtests of Arithmetic, Digit Span, and Coding). Her arithmetic scores on other tests were lower than average. Low scores on the Comprehension and Digit Span subtests indicate that memory problems may be hindering Audri. Pattern analysis at this time is highly speculative, but may be helpful in individual cases.

The next testing was achievement. This was done to see how Audri compares with other children in subjects such as reading, spelling, and arithmetic. Children often learn by fits and starts and can exhibit erratic growth patterns. Tests take this normal deviation into account so that a score outside the normal range indicates serious learning difficulties.

In reading, Audri scored at the 19th percentile on the WRAT. This means that of all children her age who took the test, her score would be higher than 19 percent of the scores and lower than 81 percent of the scores. As a rough approximation, children who score at the 16th percentile or above are able to follow the regular school curriculum. Audri's score is borderline, but several factors must be taken into consideration with this test. It is less technically adequate than recommended. This means that there could be some error present which might make Audri's true score either higher or lower than she earned on the administration of the test. Another thing to keep in mind is that this test only measures one aspect of reading (i.e., vocabulary). In spite of these apparent shortcomings, the test is widely used because it is quick and easy to give and score and yields good preliminary information. To check Audri's reading achievement more fully, the Woodcock Reading Mastery Tests and some informal measures were given. These showed that Audri has difficulty with phonics, putting sounds together to make words, and sight vocabulary. When she is anxious, she tries too hard and has difficulty with comprehension (i.e., the ability to remember facts about the story line and to recall descriptive details). She needs help in developing memory skills, word attack skills, and in relaxing so she can concentrate better. Her anxiety will probably diminish as she experiences success academically, and, at this time, no anxiety reducing activities are planned.

In handwriting, it was found that Audri gets lost because she draws the individual letters and can't concentrate on the meaning of the word or passage she is writing. In addition to teacher analysis of Audri's handwriting, comparisons were made with samples produced by other children. The Zaner-Bloser charts show that her writing approximates that of an average second grader. She needs to practice her cursive writing, learn a number of cursive letter forms, and connect the letters within each word. With practice, she can develop a smoother flow, reduce the size of each letter, and feel more comfortable with her penmanship. Eventually it should become so automatic that she will be able to think and write without being distracted by the letter formations.

In spelling, she has difficulty as shown by her score at the 12th percentile on the WRAT. This is below average and can be brought up. Because of her ability as shown by the IQ test, it can be assumed that remedial help could be beneficial in this area. The first thing to do is work on memory skills. She needs to practice her words to herself and keep doing this until she can remember the words.

Arithmetic skills are not well developed. She earned a score at the 10th percentile on the arithmetic subtest of the WRAT. The IQ test had a subtest in arithmetic. On this measure Audri scored in the average range. This kind of pattern of erratic performance is not unusual in children who are having memory problems. Other testing shows that she doesn't seem to have an idea about how to use arithmetic skills to solve problems. Again, her memory skills are hurting her. She gets lost because she has to count to get the answer to all computations and forgets where she is in the problem. The first step is to memorize some of the tables. Drill is essential.

Audri was given a perceptual test, the ITPA. This can sometimes give an indication of learning style strengths and weaknesses. The results of this test lend support to the belief that Audri is having memory problems and also indicate that her ability to learn from listening may not be as developed as her ability to learn from seeing or handling objects.

The pattern of performance as shown by the testing is not unlike that of children who have been helped by methods used for the learning disabiled. Audri has normal ability, yet is failing to achieve at the expected level in school, even though she tries. Her poorly developed auditory and memory problems seem to be hindering progress in all academic areas. Children classified as learning disabled may exhibit this type of behavior. If placed in the learning disability program, Audri will have the chance to learn ways to overcome her auditory and memory problems; these, one can hope, will help her catch up to the others in her class.

Points to Ponder

It is difficult to paraphrase a conversation between teacher and parent. This mythical explanation had no provision for parent questions. At appropriate points, the teacher must ask for and answer questions raised by parents. Even facial expressions indicating bewilderment must not go unresolved. Some parents will be satisfied with the word of a teacher that their child is having problems and should be placed in special education. Others may want to gain a complete understanding of their child's disability, including the justification for the diagnosis and the rationale for the prognosis. For the teacher, it is a much more secure feeling to go into a parent conference overprepared rather than the reverse. It is very difficult to predict the course a parent-teacher conference may take. A teacher may be asked to explain anything from the normal curve to what constitutes special education.

At a minimum, the teacher should be prepared to answer questions about technical aspects of tests, how a child could be classified through use of tests, how formal tests can be used in the construction of informal tests, and how the package can be brought together to develop the goals and objectives used in instructional programs. Because statistics are not dealt with on a daily basis, the teacher will want to periodically review concepts used in testing. A yearly review of statistics and commonly used test manuals is sufficient for many teachers.

Parents are often receptive to the explanation that their child seems to fit the pattern of certain other children, such as that of the learning disabled, educable mentally retarded, or whatever. If statements of that type are made, however, the teacher must be prepared to justify the conclusions made, even to the point of explaining the score patterns.

A very important point is that parents should leave the conference with an idea of what the testing showed and what can be done educationally to help solve the problems which the evaluation revealed. It is also very important to seek parental input. A concerned teacher asks what objectives the parents have for their child and explores ways in which the school and home will cooperate so that the most efficient instruction possible may be rendered to the child. The effort expended by the teacher (learning tests and statistics, developing instructional programs, and opening channels of communication with parents) is well worth the potential improved achievement of the student. No educational goal is greater than a student achieving to potential.

REFERENCES

Barbe, W., Lucas, H., Hackney, C., and McAllister, C. 1979. *Creative growth with handwriting,* 2nd ed. Columbus, Ohio: Zaner-Bloser.

Berger, J. H. 1981. *Parents as partners in education.* St. Louis: C. V. Mosby.

Connolly, A. J., Nachtman, W., and Pritchett, E. M. 1970. *KeyMath diagnostic arithmetic test.* Circle Pines, Minnesota: American Guidance Service.

Jastak, J. F., and Jastak, S. R. 1978. *Wide range achievement test.* Wilmington, Delaware: Jastak Associates.

Kirk, S. A., McCarthy, J. J., and Kirk, W. D. 1968. *Illinois test of psycholinguistic abilities,* rev. ed. Urbana, Illinois: University of Illinois Press.

Wechsler, D. 1974. *Wechsler intelligence scale for children—revised.* New York: Psychological Corporation.

Woodcock, R. W. 1972. *Woodcock reading mastery tests.* Circle Pines, Minnesota: American Guidance Service.

GLOSSARY

Achievement testing. The use of instruments designed to determine what a child has learned.

Age equivalent score. A derived score indicating the age group in which a child's raw test score is average.

Algorithm. A series of steps designed to solve a mathematical problem.

Alternate-forms reliability. The correlation coefficient obtained when two equivalent forms of a test are administered to the same sample.

Aptitude testing. The use of instruments designed to predict future performance in some activity or to judge the ability to learn new tasks. IQ is an example of an aptitude test.

Arithmetic mean ($\overline{X}$). The sum of the scores divided by the number of scores, often called the average. Other means are the geometric mean and the harmonic mean, which are beyond the scope of psychoeducational assessment.

Assessment. A determination based on the use of instruments and observations.

Bell-shaped curve. A set of scores which approximates the shape of a vertical cross-section of a bell in which the frequency of scores is greatest in the middle and falls off to each side in a regular fashion.

Centile. See *percentile.*

Chart. See *graph.*

Chronological age (CA). A child's calendar age, found by subtracting date of birth from the current date.

Coefficient. A value which can be thought of either as a constant or any factor of a product. In the product $4\pi r^2$, 4 and π are constants and, therefore, are coefficients. It can also be said that 4 is a coefficient of πr^2, that 4π is a coefficient of r^2, that $4r^2$ is a coefficient of π, and so on.

Coefficient of internal consistency. See *split-half reliability.*

Concurrent validitiy. A criterion-related measure in which a set of test scores gathered from a sample is correlated with another measure gathered from the same sample at approximately the same time.

Confidence interval. The range with an observed score serving as the mean in which a true score is said to be captured with some degree of certainty.

Constant. A trait or characteristic which is fixed for the sample in question. It is the opposite of a variable.

Construct validity. A judgment of how well a test measures a theory or trait or construct. Also called *logical validity.*

Content validity. A judgment of test content by independent experts to determine if a test (1) measures what has been taught, (2) includes a representative sample of items, (3) taps understanding of a skill or skills, and (4) eliminates clues which would allow correct responses to be chosen without mastery of the skill(s) being measured. Also called *curricular validity.*

Continuous measure. A number which approximates a value between two points.

Correlation. A determination of the relationship between two variables, expressed as a coefficient. Examples of correlation coefficients include the Pearson product-moment (r), Spearman rank-order (ρ), Kendall's tau (τ), phi (ϕ), tetrachoric, biserial, rank-biserial, and point-biserial.

Counter. See *unit.*

Criterion-referenced testing. A measure or measures designed to determine mastery of a task or tasks.

Criterion-related validity. The correlation of a set of test scores with another measure taken from the same sample. Criterion-related validity is subdivided into concurrent validity and predictive validity. Also called *statistical validity* and *empirical validity.*

Curricular validity. See *content validity.*

Curriculum. A series of objectives leading to the fulfillment of annual and terminal goals.

Decile. One of nine points that divide an ordered distribution of scores into ten parts of equal frequency.

Descriptive statistic. A number used to describe or summarize data.

Deviation IQ. A standard score which expresses IQ measurement with a mean of 100 and standard deviation of 15, 16, or 24.

Diagnosis. A determination of which skills the child has and has not learned.

Discrepancy. Significantly different scores within a child's test performance.

Discrete measure. A number which is limited to whole units or counters.

Dispersion. The indication of how much a set of scores deviates on each side of a measure of central tendency. Included are the range, quartile deviation (semi-interquartile range), and standard deviation. Also called *spread of scores* and *variability.*

Distribution. A table or graph used to present a picture or summary of a set of scores.

Educational programming. The planned, systematic delivery of instruction to a child.

Empirical method. The collection of data through direct observation of phenomena.

Empirical validity. See *criterion-related validity.*

Error. The difference between the obtained measure and the true measure.

Evaluation. A determination based on the use of instruments and judgment.

Examiner. One who administers and interprets the results of tests.

Extrapolation. The estimation of a value of a variable which lies beyond the range of available values.

Face validity. An extremely superficial form of content validity, often characterized by presentation of testimonials, which should not be accepted in lieu of content validity studies.

Formal testing. See *norm-referenced testing.*

Frequency (f). The number of times a score was earned in a set of scores.

Frequency distribution. A condensed list in which each score is shown once opposite the number of times that score was earned.

Frequency polygon. This is usually an arithmetic chart in which the frequency of each score is plotted and the points connected in order by straigth line segments.

Gaussian curve. See *normal curve.*

Grade equivalent score. A derived score indicating the grade group in which a child's raw test score is average.

Graph. A pictorial representation of a set of scores. Included are the frequency polygon and histogram.

Histogram. A graph used with grouped scores which takes the form of a series of rectangles.

Index of stability. See *test-retest reliability.*

Individualization of instruction. Educational programming which is tailored to the unique needs of each child.

Inferential statistic. A number used to make generalizations beyond the data at hand, estimate unknown values, or evaluate differences among groups.

Informal testing. See *criterion-referenced testing.*

Instrument. A device for gathering data, e.g., a ruler, test, and thermometer.

Intelligence quotient (IQ). A numerical indication of a child's aptitude, determined by testing.

Interpolation. The estimation of the value of a variable between two given values.

Interquartile range. A measure of dispersion about the median in which the first quartile score is subtracted from the third quartile score to obtain the range of the middle fifty percent of the scores.

Interscorer reliability. See *scorer reliability.*

Interval scale measure. An equal unit scale with an arbitrary zero point in which the measured value of an object denotes the number of units of measurement possessed by that object, associated with continuous data.

Intrascorer reliability. The correlation coefficient calculated when the scores obtained by a sample of examiners are correlated with the scores obtained by the same examiners on the same tests at a later time.

Learning style. The preferences a child shows in her attempts to acquire knowledge.

Line of best fit. A straight or curved line fitted to a distribution such that the smallest average distance from the line to each score in the distribution is obtained.

List. A table showing each score in a set of scores.

Logical validity. See *construct validity*.

Mean. See *arithmetic mean*.

Measurement. The application of an instrument to gather quantitative data, expressed as a continuous or discrete number.

Measures of central tendency. Included are the mean, median, and mode. Each is a typical value or most likely value in a set of scores.

Median (Mdn). The point at which fifty percent of the scores lie above and fifty percent lie below. The median is the midpoint in a range of scores and is equal to the fiftieth percentile.

Mental age (MA). The chronological age at which a given child's mental functioning is comparable.

Mode. The most common score in a set of scores.

Multidisciplinary team. A group of educational experts and parents formed to insure quality educational programming.

Nominal scale measure. A numerical label or measure of identity, associated with categories.

Normal curve. A bell-shaped curve in which the mean, median, and mode all fall at the same point.

Norm-referenced testing. A measure or measures designed to compare a child's performance against his peers in predetermined areas. Also called *standardized testing* and *formal testing*.

Norms. The average test performance of the standardization sample.

Ordinal scale measure. A numerical indicator of the relative quality or quantity of a given trait which objects possess, associated with ranks.

Pearson product-moment correlation coefficient (r). A numerical indication of the relationship between two variables when both are interval or ratio scale measures.

Percentage. The ratio of a score to the total number of possible items, multiplied by 100.

Percentile. One of 99 points that divide an ordered distribution of scores into 100 parts of equal frequency. Also called *centile*.

Personality testing. The use of instruments designed to determine adjustment, attitude, and interests. Adaptive behavior is measured through personality tests.

Predictive validity. A criterion-related measure in which a set of test scores gathered from a sample is correlated with another measure gathered from the same sample at a future date.

Prescription. The setting of objectives the child is to master within a given time.

Profile. The plot of scores of the subtests comprising a test or the plot of scores of several tests comprising a battery.

Psychological report. A written statement listing a child's presenting problem, test score results, interpretations, observations, conclusions, and recommendations for programming.

Quantile family. Those scores of relative standing expressed in terms of their rank in an ordered distribution. Included are the percentile or centile score, decile, and quartile.

Quartile. One of three points that divide an ordered distribution of scores into four parts of equal frequency.

Quartile deviation. A measure of dispersion about the median in which the range of the middle fifty percent of the scores in a set of scores is divided by two. Also called *semi-interquartile range.*

Radical. See *square root.*

Random sample. A part or subset of a population which has the same proportions of various traits or characteristics as that of the population.

Range. A crude measure of dispersion calculated by finding the difference between the highest score and lowest score in a set of scores.

Rapport. The degree of comfort a child feels with an examiner.

Ratio IQ. An IQ score expressed by dividing a child's mental age by his chronological age, multiplied by 100.

Ratio scale measure. An interval scale measure in which zero indicates an absence of the trait being measured, associated with continuous measurement.

Raw score. The score obtained on a test before any operations are performed on it, such as the number of correct answers on a subtest.

Regression line. A straight line fitted to a distribution such that the smallest average distance from the line to each score in the distribution is obtained.

Reliability. The degree of consistency of measurement obtained from a test instrument.

Sample (n). A part or subset of a population.

Scale. One of the four types of measurement, based on the characteristics of the data being collected. The scales are nominal, ordinal, interval, and ratio.

Scorer reliability. The correlation coefficient calculated when two sets of examiners score the same set of test data.

Scores of relative standing. Those scores described by their relationship to other scores in a normal distribution. Included are standard scores and the quantile family.

Self-concept. How a child perceives herself.

Semi-interquartile range. See *quartile deviation.*

Sigma (Σ). The uppercase Greek letter used to denote the sum of a group of scores.

Sigma score formula. A method for converting one standard score to another, such as a *z*-score to a *T*-score.

Slope. The rate of change of a line or curve with respect to its vertical and horizontal axes.

Smooth curve. A curve in which minor fluctuations have been eliminated.

Smoothing. The process by which a histogram or frequency polygon is transformed through fitting a curved line to the figure.

Spearman rank-order correlation coeffieicnt (ρ). A numerical indication of the relationship between two variables when both are ordinal scale measures.

Split-half reliability. The correlation coefficient obtained when a test is administered to a sample and one-half of the items in each test are correlated with the other half.

Spread of scores. See *dispersion.*

Square. The value which results when a number is multiplied by itself.

Square root. A number which, when multiplied by itself, yields the original value. Also called *radical.*

Standard deviation (SD). The average of the degree to which a set of scores deviates from the mean in a normal distribution.

Standard error. The standard deviation of the sampling distribution of a statistic.

Standard error of estimate. The standard deviation of the distribution of error around a regression line.

Standard error of measurement (SEM). The standard deviation of the distribution of error around an obtained score.

Standard scores. Those scores of relative standing expressed in terms of their linear distance from the mean in a normal distribution. Included are the *z*-score, *T*-score, deviation IQ, and stanine.

Standardized testing. See *norm-referenced testing.*

Standardization. The process of eliminating ambiguity in the administration, scoring, and interpretation of tests.

Stanine. A standard score with nine intervals.

Statistic. A number used to summarize, analyze, or evaluate data collected from a sample. A statistic may be descriptive or inferential.

Statistical validitiy. See *criterion-related validity.*

Stigma. The negative bias exhibited toward a child which can result after the child is assigned a label, such as mentally retarded or emotionally disturbed.

Tangent. The stright line which touches a curved line at one and only one point on that curved line.

Test protocol. The procedure used to administer a test, including the form, blank, answer sheet, or record.

Test-retest reliability. A measure of self-correlation in which the correlation coefficient of two sets of test scores is calculated. Each set consists of an administration of the test to the same sample separated by a time interval.

Test scatter. The pattern of subtest score differences of a child.

Testing. A measurement of what a child can and cannot do in the cognitive, affective, or psychomotor domains at any given time, usually through use of aptitude, achievement, or personality instruments.

Total test score. A single score derived from a group of subtest scores.

T-score. A standard score with a mean of 50 and standard deviation of 10.

Unit. A single, indivisible entity which can be thought of as a fixed quantity or amount. Also called *counter.*

Validity. The degree to which a test measures what its authors or users claim it measures. Measures of test validity include concurrent validity, construct validity, and content validity.

Variability. See *dispersion.*

Variable. A trait or characteristic which can take on more than one value in a sample, usually expressed as a letter.

z-score. A standard score with a mean of zero and standard deviation of one.

953